Letts

Framework
FOCUS

Poetry

Christopher Martin

Published by Letts Educational
The Chiswick Centre
414 Chiswick High Road
London W4 5TF

📞 020 89963333
📠 020 87428390
✉ mail@lettsed.co.uk
🌐 www.letts-education.com

Letts Educational Limited is a division of Granada Learning Limited, part of Granada plc.

© Christopher Martin 2003

First published 2003

ISBN 1 84085 8796

British Library Cataloguing in Publication Data

A catalogue record for this book is available from the British Library.

Developed and packaged by McLean Press Ltd

Commissioned by Helen Clark

Project management by Vicky Butt

Edited by Sue Gardner

Cover design by bigtop, Bicester, UK

Internal design by bigtop, Bicester, UK

Illustrations by James Arnold, Paul McCaffrey, Linda Combi and Rosalind Hudson.

Production by PDQ

Printed and bound by Canale, Italy

Literacy Credits

Contents

Introduction

What use are poets? Surely people who do real jobs to keep the world going are more important? Yet, strangely, however good and caring their work, people who do 'real' jobs are gradually forgotten but the best poets live on, rediscovered and enjoyed by each generation.

Francis Thompson (1859–1907), a Victorian poet who seemed so useless that he slept rough on London's streets, wrote a poem about this contrast. He looked at poppies in a cornfield. He saw himself as the poppy (a weed known for its dream inducing qualities) and the ordinary working world as the wheat.

> I hang, 'mid men my needless head,
> And my fruit is dreams, as theirs is bread:
> The goodly men and the sun-hazed sleeper
> Time shall reap, but after the reaper
> The world shall glean of me, the sleeper.

Dreams (or ideas), he says, last longer than daily bread. When we have done our jobs, shopped and eaten our meals, then we start to think – about our relationships, time passing, the natural world, children, the seasons, animals, war and peace, where we come from, what happens after death... The great poets find wonderful words to talk about these great human interests, and that is why they are important to us.

There are poems here from different cultures, and different times – some were written 2000 years ago, others were published recently. There are men's and women's voices. Some of the more famous poets appear on the National Curriculum set or recommended author lists. As the English Framework requires, you can find out here *how* poets write, and about those technical terms that you should know and be able to apply, such as form, imagery, and meter.

You have covered a good range of poems in Key Stage 2. Here are more: some straightforward, others demanding – all are memorable. There are activities for you to do individually, or with a partner or group, and as spoken or written work. The homework sections offer chances for extended imaginative, analytical or comparative responses. When you write your answers, remember to take your paragraph structure and take illustrative quotations from the poems themselves. Try to use technical language to discuss poetry: the glossary will help.

A close study of these units will help prepare you for the SATs, and give you excellent grounding for English studies at GCSE.

KS2 review

Making poetry is one of the most exciting things that people do with language. Studying, and writing, poetry is therefore at the heart of your English work.

If you have followed the National Literacy programme in Years 5 and 6, you will have been introduced to a wide range of poetry material. You have been taught how to respond to it, and, of course, you tried writing your own poems – often the most enjoyable and creative way to learn about poetry.

Your programme was ambitious. You had to cover poems
● by famous, long-established authors
● by significant children's writers
● by poets from different cultures.

You also learned about various forms of poetry:
● ballad
● sonnet
● elegy
● narrative poem
● rap
● nonsense verse
● concrete poem
● haiku.

You found out about the different features of each form. You tried your hand at writing them, by filling in gaps in a given poem, by writing an additional stanza or two, or, for example, by composing your own haiku sequence.

Then, of course, there were the technical words that you need to discuss poems:
● simile
● metaphor
● personification
● rhyme
● rhythm
● assonance
● alliteration etc.

Perhaps you looked closely at the work of one poet, or compared and contrasted the themes and styles of several poets together. You began to explore and interpret the layers of meanings in poems, and how poets convey moods, feelings and attitudes.

You may have made an anthology of poems that you personally enjoy, adding commentaries to explain what you liked about your chosen pieces. Or, apart from writing, you may have tried performing poems, working out, in groups, how to read them dramatically together – that can be exciting!

The best part of poetry study is discovering those magical poems that everyone loves: De la Mare's 'The listeners', Causley's 'Timothy Winters', Noyes's 'The highwayman', Lear's 'The Jumblies', Browning's 'The Pied Piper of Hamelin', Yeats's 'The lake isle of Innisfree', or a sonnet by Shakespeare. Or you may have followed selections in one of the good Key Stage 2 anthologies, like *Teaching poetry* by Louise Fidge (Letts).

This book builds on what you have learned, and carries you forward. Your interests, and your skills in reading and writing, grow quickly as you get older, and the poems and exercises in this collection will stimulate those interests and challenge those skills.

Some people think that poetry is old-fashioned and out-moded, and that film, television, and the internet have somehow taken its place. This is untrue. Poetry is based on basic human interests and instincts that never change, and it is always being reborn, as the recently written poems in this collection will show you. Years ago Elizabeth Barrett Browning (1806–1861), the famous Victorian poet said the same thing. She refused to believe, as people said in her time, 'that poetry was worn out for ever – as if the morning star was worn out from heaven, or the yellow primrose from the grass'.

Simple pleasures

Aims

- To engage with, and make sense of, poems.
- To recognise how writers' language choices can enhance meaning.

Starter session

There are many expensive pleasures in life: exotic holidays, fast cars, designer clothes. There are also simple pleasures that cost nothing: a fine sunset, spring flowers appearing, a rainbow… Work with a partner and make a list of six things that give pleasure and which cost nothing (include people and pets as well as the natural world). Read your list to the class.

Introduction

Rupert Brooke (1887–1915) was very famous in his day and is now best known for the **sonnets** that he wrote just before his death in the First World War:

> If I should die, think only this of me:
> That there's some corner of a foreign field
> That is for ever England […]

Development

A **SPEAKING AND LISTENING** **READING** **WRITING**

In this activity, you are going to look closely at a poem by Rupert Brooke. He wrote 'The great lover' in 1914. His title is sarcastic: he is not discussing human love but those little free things that he enjoys in life. Here is part of the poem.

FROM THE GREAT LOVER

[...] These I have loved:

            White plates and cups, clean-gleaming,
Ringed with blue lines ; and feathery, faery dust ;
Wet roofs, beneath the lamp-light ; the strong crust
Of friendly bread ; and many tasting food ;
Rainbows ; and the blue bitter smoke of wood ;
And radiant raindrops couching in cool flowers ;
And flowers themselves, that sway through sunny hours,
Dreaming of moths that drink them under the moon ;
Then, the cool kindliness of sheets, that soon
Smooth away trouble ; and the rough male kiss
Of blankets ; grainy wood ; live hair that is
Shining and free ; blue-massing clouds ; the keen
Unpassioned beauty of a great machine ;
The benison of hot water ; furs to touch ;
The good smell of old clothes ; and other such—
The comfortable smell of friendly fingers,
Hair's fragrance, and the musty reek that lingers
About dead leaves and last year's ferns. [...]
            Dear names,

And thousand other throng to me ! Royal flames ;
Sweet water's dimpling laugh from tap or spring ;
Holes in the ground ; and voices that do sing ;
Voices in laughter, too ; and body's pain,
Soon turned to peace ; and the deep-panting train ;
Firm sands ; and the little dulling edge of foam
That browns and dwindles as the wave goes home ;
And washen stones, gay for an hour ; the cold
Graveness of iron ; moist black earthen mould ;
Sleep ; and high places ; footprints in the dew ;
And oaks ; and brown horse-chestnuts, glossy-new ;
And new-peeled sticks ; and shining pools on grass;—
All these have been my loves. [...]

Vocabulary

benison: blessing

washen stones: sea washed pebbles

The poem is a kind of list, divided by semi-colons. Work with a partner to discuss the following.

1 Which items do you agree with? With which do you disagree?

2 Which seem old-fashioned or just strange?

3 What is the point of 'dear names'?

4 Some items are single words: sleep, rainbows, etc. Some have delicately-chosen **adjectives** to define them. On your own, list some of these that you find effective and then discuss your choice with your partner.

5 Some items contain **metaphors**. Find some of these with your partner.

You are going to consider how **diction** and **comparisons** can enhance meaning. Martin Armstrong (1882–1967) was another First World War poet. In 'The Senses' he describes how the soul develops 'From the worlds' odours, sights and sounds'.

Vocabulary

tepid: warm	
share: plough blade	
cleaves: cuts	
riven: torn	
eighteen-pounders: field guns	
Tuscan: from Tuscany, Italy	

Armstrong imitates Brooke's list effect but he includes longer, more fully defined items. There are three sections here: scents, sights, sounds.

1 On your own, look carefully at the adjectives, **verbs** and comparisons Armstrong uses. List them in a table.

2 Choose one item from each section where you particularly like the language choices. Explain to your partner why you have chosen these.

FROM THE SENSES

[...] From the perfume acrid-sweet of dead leaves burning
When autumn sunsets into dusk are turning;
    From the breath of damp stone floors
And paraffin pervading the cool porches
    And aisles of village churches;
From the tepid, flat, mechanic exhalations
    Of comfortless tube stations; [...]
Such smells as these; and of the sights,
    The gleam on blue May nights
Of the young moon in high, ancestral boughs
    Among the scant young leaves;
And in the wake of the moving ploughs
The shining earth that, as the straight share cleaves,
Turns flowingly over;
And the rosy apple-blossom on the bent
And knotted bough against the blue of heaven; [...]
        [...] And of things heard,
The cooling whisper of summer breezes sweeping
The grey-green barley-fields; and the echoes stirred
By music interwoven in some dim-lighted
Cavernous cathedral; and the eighteen-pounders'
Buoyant drumbeats and hisses and whoops united
In a hurricane barrage; and the clear laughter and shouting
Of girls in old green gardens playing rounders; [...]

Review

Read this tiny poem by the American, Raymond Carver (1939–1988). As a class, discuss what this is about. How does it fit the theme of 'simple pleasures'?

QUIET NIGHTS

I go to sleep on one beach,
wake up on another.

Boat all fitted out,
tugging against its rope.

Homework

1 Which do you prefer, the Brooke or the Armstrong poem extract? Say what each is about and then try to explain your preference, looking closely at the items chosen, the diction, and the comparisons.

2 Explore the idea of simple pleasures in your own list poem. Bring in detail from all five of your senses. Use the semi-colon dividers. Include up-to-date things – the world has changed since the two poets were writing!

Ballads

Aims

- To understand that ballads have been important in the literary heritage.
- To distinguish between the attitudes of characters and poet.

Starter session

The **ballad** is a special kind of **narrative poem**. It has a particular **verse form**. Here are two **stanzas** from 'The wife of Usher's Well'. As a class, read the lines and work out:

- the **rhyme scheme**
- the **rhythm**: how many **stresses** there are in each line and whether they form a pattern.

There lived a wife at Usher's Well,
    And a wealthy wife was she;
She had three stout and stalwart sons,
    And sent them o'er the sea.

They hadna been a week from her,
    A week but barely ane,
When word came to the carline wife
    That her three sons were gane. [...]

(Note: Later in the poem the sons come home as ghosts!)

Vocabulary

carline: country

Introduction

The finest ballads probably date from Shakespeare's time and were composed by anonymous minstrels working at great houses in the Border country between England and Scotland (that explains the Scottish language you often see in them). They were probably sung or chanted as part of an evening's entertainment.

Love, murder, ghosts and mystery are their favourite **themes**, or as William Wordsworth (1770–1850) said:

Old unhappy, far-off things,
    And battles long ago.

Thomas Percy (1729–1811) collected them together from an old manuscript that he discovered, and they have become a powerful part of our literature, imitated by many other poets.

Development

SPEAKING AND LISTENING   **READING**   WRITING

You are going to look at a dark murder mystery ballad where the poet allows the two characters to speak for themselves.

Read the opening of the ballad with a partner. One of you should be Edward, the other mother. Who says which lines?

Vocabulary

brand: sword

gang: go

nae mair: no more

steed: horse

erst: before

auld:old

dule ye dree: grief you suffer

wae: woe (sadness)

(The 'O' is a singing effect. The second line has only two stresses, which is unusual in a ballad.) Discuss these questions.

1 The mother sees blood on the son's sword. What two excuses does he give for it?

2 What is the terrible truth?

EDWARD, EDWARD

'WHY does your brand sae drop wi' blude,
          Edward, Edward?
Why does your brand sae drop wi' blude,
          And why sae sad gang ye, O?'
'O I hae killed my hawk sae gude,
          Mither, mither;
O I hae killed my hawk sae gude,
          And I had nae mair but he, O.'

'Your hawk's blude was never sae red,
          Edward, Edward;
Your hawk's blude was never sae red,
          My dear son, I tell thee, O.'
'O I hae killed my red-roan steed,
          Mither, mither;
O I hae killed my red-roan steed,
          That erst was sae fair and free, O.'

Your steed was auld, and ye hae got mair,
          Edward, Edward;
Your steed was auld, and ye hae got mair;
          Some other dule ye dree, O.'
'O I hae killed my father dear,
          Mither, mither;
O I hae killed my father dear,
          Alas, and wae is me, O!'

Now look at another famous ballad. 'I', the vague listener, is a typical figure in ballads. The horrible story is told by two speaking crows. Read the ballad with your partner. Discuss the questions.

THE TWA CORBIES

As I was walking all alane,
I heard twa corbies making a mane;
The tane unto the t'other say,
'Where sall we gang and dine to-day?'

'In behint yon auld fail dyke,
I wot there lies a new slain knight;
And naebody kens that he lies there,
But his hawk, his hound, and lady fair.

'His hound is to the hunting gane,
His hawk to fetch the wild-fowl hame,
His lady's ta'en another mate,
So we may mak our dinner sweet.

'Ye'll sit on his white hause-bane,
And I'll pike out his bonny blue een;
Wi ae lock o his gowden hair
We'll theek our nest when it grows bare.

'Mony a one for him makes mane,
But nane sall ken where he is gane;
Oer his white banes, when they are bare,
The wind sall blaw for evermair.'

1 What have they found?

2 Who else knows about this?

3 What will the crows do to the dead man?

4 Who is actually responsible for his death?

5 How was the murder done, do you think?

Vocabulary

twa: two

corbies: crows

mane: moan

tane: one

gang: go

auld fail dyke: old turf bank

wot: know

kens: knows

hause-bane: neck bone

bonny: beautiful

een: eyes

wi ae lock: with a strand

gowden: golden

theek: thatch

'The unquiet grave' is more restrained as a story and more English in its language. Again, no one knows who wrote it. Read the ballad. Work out who the two speakers are and which lines are spoken by which person. Make notes on the answers to the questions.

1 What has happened to the girl?

2 What is her advice to him?

3 How does she use the idea of flowers to make him accept her death?

Vocabulary

unquiet: restless

crave: beg

THE UNQUIET GRAVE

'The wind doth blow today, my love,
    And a few small drops of rain;
I never had but one true-love,
    In cold grave she was lain.

'I'll do as much for my true-love
    As any young man may;
I'll sit and mourn all at her grave
    For a twelvemonth and a day.'

The twelvemonth and a day being up,
    The dead began to speak:
'Oh who sits weeping on my grave,
    And will not let me sleep?'

'Tis I, my love, sits on your grave,
    And will not let you sleep;
For I crave one kiss of your clay-cold lips,
    And that is all I seek.'

'You crave one kiss of my clay-cold lips;
    But my breath smells earthy strong;
If you have one kiss of my clay-cold lips,
    Your time will not be long.

'Tis down in yonder garden green,
    Love, where we used to walk,
The finest flower that ere was seen
    Is withered to a stalk.

'The stalk is withered dry, my love,
    So will our hearts decay;
So make yourself content, my love,
    Till God calls you away.'

Review

Let us return to 'Edward, Edward'. Later in the poem Edward plans to leave the country. 'And what about me?' asks mother. Another dark secret is then revealed. What is it?

[…] 'The curse of hell frae me sall ye bear,
    Mither, mither,
The curse of hell frae me sall ye bear:
    Sic counsels ye gave to me, O!'

Vocabulary

sic counsels: sick advice

Discuss why Edward may have killed his father.

Homework

1 Tell the full story of the dead man in 'The twa corbies'. Include detail from the poem but also invent more background, especially about the scheming wife at home in the great house.

2 Tell the story of 'The unquiet grave', including the weird conversation at the grave-side but also filling in more detail about the relationship.

Haunted houses

Aims

- To see how poets convey setting and mood through word choice and sentence structure.
- To recognise how poets' language choices can enhance meanings.

Starter session

There are no such things as ghosts or haunted houses but they are exciting to read about. Clever writers are able to make you feel that their **settings** are sinister or threatening. Imagine entering a haunted house.
What would you expect to see, hear and touch around you?
Write a short poem using this structure:

I see …
I hear …
I touch …

Share your poem with
a small group.

Introduction

Thomas Hood (1799–1845) enjoyed ghostly tales like his friend, Charles Dickens, the novelist. In 1843, Hood visited Edinburgh Castle and saw the room where David Rizzio, a favourite courtier of Mary, Queen of Scots, was murdered. He was inspired to write a **narrative poem** about a haunted house where someone had been put to death:

> What shrieking spirit in that bloody room
> Its mortal frame had violently quitted?—

In this lesson's activities, you are going to explore how Hood and other poets convey setting and mood through word choice and sentence structure.

Development

SPEAKING AND LISTENING **READING WRITING**

On your own, read some episodes from this poem about an 'old deserted mansion' that no one dares to enter and write your answers to the questions that follow each section.

1 What signs of decay show that the house has been unused for years?

2 What do you *not* see as you look at the building?

3 What does the house make you feel?

The poet crosses the deserted garden and approaches the front doo

FROM **THE HAUNTED HOUSE**

Unhinged the iron gates half open hung,
Jarr'd by the gusty gales of many winters,
That from its crumbled pedestal had flung
One marble globe in splinters.

No human figure stirr'd, to go or come,
No face look'd forth from shut or open casement;
No chimney smoked—there was no sign of Home
From parapet to basement.

With shatter'd panes the grassy court was starr'd;
The time-worn coping-stone had tumbled after;
And thro' the ragged roof the sky shone, barr'd
With naked beam and rafter.

O'er all there hung a shadow and a fear;
A sense of mystery the spirit daunted,
And said, as plain as whisper in the ear,
The place is Haunted! [...]

Vocabulary

casement: window

The pear and quince lay squander'd on the grass;
The mould was purple with unheeded showers
Of bloomy plums—a Wilderness it was
Of fruits, and weeds, and flowers!

The fountain was a-dry—neglect and time
Had marr'd the work of artisan and mason,
And efts and croaking frogs, begot of slime,
Sprawl'd in the ruin'd bason.

The Statue, fallen from its marble base,
Amidst the refuse leaves, and herbage rotten,
Lay like the Idol of some by-gone race,
Its name and rites forgotten.

On ev'ry side the aspect was the same,
All ruined, desolate, forlorn, and savage. [...]

Vocabulary

eft: newt

begot: born

Hood chooses words to express the neglect and waste of this great house and garden. Find some of these.

He also selects words that have a sinister feel – like 'winding-sheet'. Find some others.

The centipede along the threshold crept,
The cobweb hung across in mazy tangle,
And in its winding-sheet the maggot slept,
At every nook and angle. [...]

Now read what Hood finds as he climbs the 'gloomy stairs'. The tension mounts as he draws nearer to the murder room.

Vocabulary

mazy: twisting and turning

coursed: run

The tempest with its spoils had drifted in,
Till each unwholesome stone was darkly spotted,
As thickly as the leopard's dappled skin,
With leaves that rankly rotted.

The air was thick—and in the upper gloom
The bat—or something in its shape—was winging;
And on the wall, as chilly as a tomb,
The Death's-Head moth was clinging.

Such omens in the place there seem'd to be,
At ev'ry crooked turn, or on the landing,
The straining eyeball was prepared to see
Some Apparition standing.

4 What 'omens' does he see? Why is 'something' so chilling?

5 What simile is applied to the moth?

6 What do you expect to see on the landing?

Finally he enters the 'ghostly chamber', centre of the haunting, shunned even by insects.
This was where the murder happened.

7 What signs are left of the murder?

8 What impression do you get of the victim's last moment

9 Which simile is used to describe the victim?

10 What does Hood think that he sees in the sunbeam?

And yet no gory stain was on the quilt—
The pillow in its place had slowly rotted;
The floor alone retain'd the trace of guilt,
Those boards obscurely spotted.

Obscurely spotted to the door, and thence
With mazy doubles to the grated casement—
Oh what a tale they told of fear intense,
Of horror and amazement!

What human creature in the dead of night
Had cours'd like hunted hare that cruel dista
Had sought the door, the window in his fligh
Striving for dear existence?

Across the sunbeam, with a sudden gloom,
A ghostly shadow flitted.

Atmosphere in writing means the mood conveyed by the setting. It is created by details observed through the five senses:

● vivid adjectives
● well-chosen **adverbs** and verbs
● some sharp comparisons.

Vocabulary

tempest: storm

omens: signs of evil

apparition: ghost

Look back over the poem extracts. Where do you find good examples of these points? Which passage do you find most atmospheric? Discuss with a partner.

In this activity, you will look at how language choices can enhance meaning. Some say that Hood was influenced by 'Mariana', a poem by Alfred Tennyson (1809–1892). It is about a woman who lives a lonely life in an isolated 'moated grange'. She is waiting for her lover to visit her but he never comes… Read the poem extract and then discuss the questions with a partner.

Vocabulary

wainscot: wall panels
crevice: mouse-hole

1 Mariana is haunted by unhappiness rather than ghosts. Yet one passage is rather ghostly. Where is this?

2 Where are sounds and tiny details of what you see used to make atmosphere?

FROM MARIANA

With blackest moss the flower-plots
  Were thickly crusted, one and all:
The rusted nails fell from the knots
  That held the pear to the gable-wall.
The broken sheds looked sad and strange:
  Unlifted was the clinking latch;
Weeded and worn the ancient thatch
  Upon the lonely moated grange.
    She only said, 'My life is dreary,
      He cometh not,' she said;
    She said, 'I am aweary, aweary,
      I would that I were dead!' […]

All day within the dreamy house,
  The doors upon their hinges creaked;
The blue fly sung in the pane; the mouse
  Behind the mouldering wainscot shrieked,
Or from the crevice peered about.
  Old faces glimmered through the doors,
  Old footsteps trod the upper floors,
Old voices called her from without.
    She only said, 'My life is dreary,
      He cometh not,' she said;
    She said, 'I am aweary, aweary,
      I would that I were dead!' […]

Review

How are Mariana's fading hopes seen in the decaying house around her? Discuss together.

Homework

Write Hood's diary entry about his visit to his imagined haunted house. Make it mysterious and chilling. Use details from the extracts but add your own ideas too.

Beowulf

Aims

- To recognise how poets' language choices can enhance meaning.
- To explore the idea of literary heritage and why some works have been influential.

Starter session

The Angles and Saxons, coming from north Germany, invaded and settled in England between the fourth and seventh centuries. They created their own literature.

A **verse form** that they enjoyed was the riddle. Here is an example.

Discuss what you think it is about with a partner.

RIDDLE 1

Abandoned unborn by my begetters
I was still dead a few spring days ago:
no beat in the breast, no breath in me.

A kinswoman covered me in the clothes she wore,
no kind but kind indeed. I was coddled & swaddled
as close as I had been a baby of her own,
until, as had been shaped, so shielded, though no kin,
the unguessed guest grew great with life.

She fended for me, fostered me, she fed me up,
till I was of a size to set my bounds
further afield. She had fewer dear
sons and daughters because she did so.

Introduction

Beowulf is the greatest piece of Anglo-Saxon poetry. It was probably composed by an anonymous minstrel-poet in the seventh century but written down by a monk in about AD1000. The **manuscript** survives (though it was slightly scorched in a fire in 1731) in the British Library.

It tells the story of a fifth- or sixth-century Scandinavian hero, Beowulf. He faces two formidable challenges: the monster Grendel, whom he defeats, and a fire-dragon, which he kills, but dies in the process.

Development

To explore the idea of literary heritage, you will look at two translations of the same episode in *Beowulf*. (The original Anglo-Saxon is too different from modern English for us to follow easily.)

Hrothgar, King of the Danes, has a splendid gold-decorated Hall, Heorot. It has been attacked repeatedly by Grendel, who kills and eats its defenders. Beowulf, a Swedish hero, volunteers to help. He and his men wait in the Hall for Grendel's night attack. In the activities, you will look at how language can enhance meaning.

A **SPEAKING AND LISTENING   READING   WRITING**

The first translation is by Kevin Crossley-Holland (b 1941). Read the poem and then discuss the questions in a small group. Feed back your answers to the class.

FROM 'BEOWULF'

[…] Then, under night's shroud, Grendel walked down
from the moors; he shouldered God's anger […]
He strode under the skies, until he stood
before the feasting-hall, in front of the gift-building
gleaming with gold […]
                              The outer door, bolted
with iron bands, burst open at a touch from his hands:
with evil in his mind, and overriding anger,
Grendel swung open the hall's mouth itself. At once,
seething with fury, the fiend stepped onto
the tessellated floor; a horrible light,
like a lurid flame, flickered in his eyes.
He saw many men, a group of warriors,
a knot of kinsmen, sleeping in the hall.
His spirit leapt, his heart laughed;
the savage monster planned to sever,
before daybreak, the life of every warrior
from his body—he fully expected to eat
his fill at the feast […]
[…] for a start, he hungrily seized
a sleeping warrior, greedily wrenched him,
bit into his body, drank the blood
from his veins, devoured huge pieces;
until, in no time, he had swallowed the whole man,
even his feet and hands.

Vocabulary

tesselated: mosaic

lurid: ghastly

1 How are Grendel's strength and size indicated here?

2 Find some words that show his violence and aggression.

FROM 'BEOWULF'

[...] In off the moors, down through the mist-bands
God-cursed Grendel came greedily loping.
The bane of the race of men roamed forth,
hunting for a prey in the high hall.
Under the cloud-murk he moved towards it
until it shone above him, a sheer keep
of fortified gold. [...]
                        The iron-braced door
turned on its hinge when his hands touched it.
Then his rage boiled over, he ripped open
the mouth of the building, maddening for blood,
pacing the length of the patterned floor
with his loathsome tread, while a baleful light,
flame more than light, flared from his eyes.
He saw many men in the mansion, sleeping,
a ranked company of kinsmen and warriors
quartered together. And his glee was demonic,
picturing the mayhem: before morning
he would rip life from limb and devour them,
feed on their flesh...
...he grabbed and mauled a man on his bench,
bit into his bone-lappings, bolted down his blood
and gorged on him in lumps, leaving the body
utterly lifeless, eaten up
hand and foot.

Vocabulary

keep: stronghold

mayhem: violence

bone-lappings: joints

The second translation is by Seamus Heaney (b 1939), who won the Nobel Prize for Literature in 1995. Read the poem on your own and then write the answers to the questions.

1 The Anglo-Saxons did not use rhyme and rhythm. They liked **alliterative** verse, where the line is held together by repeating the same sounds at the beginning of words:

'flame more than light, flared from his eyes'

Copy the first four lines of Heaney's translation, and mark the **alliteration**.

2 Make two columns and collect words and **phrases** describing Grendel from the two passages. Look particularly for **verbs**. Which description is more impressive?

3 Look at the conclusion of both translations where Grendel eats the Swedish warrior. Compare the details and the language. Which is more dramatic?

Review

Try another Anglo-Saxon riddle from the eighth-century 'Exeter Book'

Discuss what this is!

Vocabulary

ornate: decorated

RIDDLE 2

The wave, over the wave, a weird thing I saw,
thorough-wrought, and wonderfully ornate:
a wonder on the wave – water become bone.

Homework

Grendel is a disappointingly vague figure. He seems to have human shape (but larger), with claws, scaled skin and glowing eyes. He lives in an underwater cave.

Use details from the passage (and a thesaurus) to make your own description of Grendel. Include some good comparisons to describe Grendel.

Cowper's hares

Aims

- To study poetry that relates to our own experience.
- To see how writers' language enhances meaning.

Starter session

Animals can be very important in our lives. Vets tell us that keeping pets is good for human beings. Put up your hand and suggest various reasons why this is so.

Introduction

William Cowper (1731–1800) was a poet and hymn-writer. Mental illness forced him to stop being a London lawyer and he retired to a quiet country life at Olney, Buckinghamshire. He was looked after by a kindly widow, Mary Unwin, who encouraged him to write, to walk, and to garden to distract him from the stress that caused his breakdowns. His most delightful distractions were his pet hares, Puss, Tiney and Bess (all males). He described them in a magazine.

Development

A **SPEAKING AND LISTENING   READING   WRITING**

In this activity, you will see how a writer's language enhances meaning. As a class, read these extracts from Cowper's article.

'Puss grew presently familiar, would leap into my lap, raise himself upon his hinder feet, and bite the hair from my temples. He would suffer me to take him up and carry him about in my arms, and has more than once fallen asleep upon my knee. He was ill three days, during which time I nursed him [...] and, by constant care and trying him with a variety of herbs, restored him to perfect health. No creature could be more grateful than my patient after his recovery; a sentiment which he expressed, by licking my hand, first the back of it, then the palm, then every finger separately, then between all the fingers [...] I made it my custom to carry him always after breakfast into the garden, where he hid himself generally under the leaves of a cucumber vine, sleeping or chewing the cud till evening [...] He would invite me to the garden by drumming upon my knee [...] If this did not immediately succeed, he would take the skirt of my coat between his teeth, and pull at it with all his force.

Upon Tiney the kindest treatment had not the least effect. He too was sick, and in his sickness had an equal share of my attention; but if, after his recovery I took the liberty to stroke him, he would grunt, strike with his fore feet, spring forward and bite. He was, however, very entertaining in his way, even his surliness was a matter of mirth, and in his play he preserved such a solemnity of manner, that in him too I had an agreeable companion.

Bess, who died soon after he was full grown, and whose death was occasioned by his being turned into his box which had been washed, while it was yet damp, was a hare of great humour and drollery [...] Bess had a courage and a confidence that made him tame from the beginning.

I always admitted them into the parlour after supper, when the carpet affording their feet a firm hold, they would frisk and bound and play a thousand gambols, in which Bess, being remarkably strong and fearless, was always superior to the rest [...] One evening the cat being in the room had the hardiness to pat Bess upon the cheek, an indignity which he resented by drumming upon her back with such violence, that the cat was happy to escape from under his paws and hide herself.'

As a class, make notes on the behaviour and 'characters' of the three pet hares. Discuss which one would you prefer as a pet.

Vocabulary

surliness: bad temper

drollery: fun

In this activity, you will look at a poem that may relate to your own experience. When Tiney died, Cowper wrote an **epitaph** for him. Read this as a class.

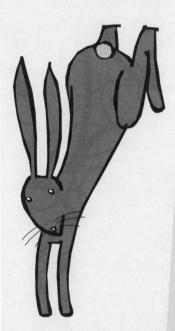

EPITAPH ON A HARE

Here lies, whom hound did ne'er pursue,
　　Nor swifter greyhound follow,
Whose foot ne'er tainted morning dew,
　　Nor ear heard huntsman's hallo,

Old Tiney, surliest of his kind,
　　Who, nurs'd with tender care,
And to domestic bounds confin'd,
　　Was still a wild Jack-hare.

Though duly from my hand he took
　　His pittance ev'ry night,
He did it with a jealous look,
　　And, when he could, would bite.

His diet was of wheaten bread,
　　And milk, and oats, and straw,
Thistles, or lettuces instead,
　　With sand to scour his maw.

On twigs of hawthorn he regal'd,
　　On pippins' russet peel;
And, when his juicy salads fail'd,
　　Sliced carrot pleased him well.

A Turkey carpet was his lawn,
　　Whereon he loved to bound,
To skip and gambol like a fawn,
　　And swing his rump around.

His frisking was at evening hours,
　　For then he lost his fear;
But most before approaching show'rs,
　　Or when a storm drew near.

Eight years and five round rolling moons
    He thus saw steal away,
Dozing out all his idle noons,
    And every night at play.

I kept him for his humour's sake,
    For he would oft beguile
My heart of thoughts that made it ache,
    And force me to a smile.

But now, beneath this walnut-shade
    He finds his long, last home,
And waits in snug concealment laid,
    Till gentler Puss shall come.

He, still more aged, feels the shocks
    From which no care can save,
And, partner once of Tiney's box,
    Must soon partake his grave.

Discuss these questions with a partner.

1 Some of the poem is written in a jokey, grand style, as if Tiney is a great hero. But some lines are simple and strongly felt. Find examples of these.

2 Where is the language most **emotive**?

3 There is a simple **rhyme scheme** (ABAB). Where do these rhymes have most force?

4 Which **stanza** tells us how Tiney helped Cowper to escape his depression?

5 Compare the prose and verse descriptions of Tiney. What extra details of him do you learn from the poem?

Vocabulary

tainted:	left a scent
Jack:	male
pittance:	share of food
scour his maw:	clean out his stomach
regaled:	enjoyed eating
russet:	red
beguile:	charm away
partake:	share

Review

As a class, compare the prose and verse descriptions of the hares. Which is more memorable? Try to explain exactly why.

Homework

1 Compose epitaphs for Bess and Puss. Take details from the prose passage. A simple way would be to write acrostics, using the hares' names. Or you could try rhymed stanzas like Cowper's. There are four **stresses** in the first line and three in the second.

2 Compose an epitaph for your pet if you have one!

Chinese poems

Aims

- To study how poets convey setting, character and mood through word choice and sentence structure.
- To explore how form contributes to meaning in poems from different times and cultures.

Starter session

Ancient China had an advanced and sophisticated society. The rule of the Tang family (618–906) created a Golden Age of Chinese poetry and art.

Here is a ninth-century poem about war by Tu Fu:

As a class, discuss how you read this poem. What does it say about war?

WAR

Blue White	Smoke Bones	War Men

Introduction

Arthur Waley (1889–1966) is the best-known translator of Chinese poetry. He learned the language when he got a job at the British Museum. He found that there were thousands of Chinese poems unknown to English readers. His best-selling '170 Chinese poems' appeared in 1918.

Development

A **SPEAKING AND LISTENING** **READING** WRITING

In this activity you will look at how poets convey setting, character and mood through word choice and sentence structure. In this poem a man mourns his dead girlfriend. Waley decided not to use **rhyme** in his translations. There are lots of rhymes in Chinese but not so many in English. With a partner, compare two translations to see if he was wise.

THE SOUND OF HER SILK SKIRT

1

The sound of her silk skirt has stopped.
On the marble pavement dust grows.
Her empty room is cold and still.
Fallen leaves are piled against the doors.
      Longing for that lovely lady
How can I bring my aching heart to rest?

(Arthur Waley)

2

The sound of rustling silk is stilled,
With dust the marble courtyard filled;
No footfalls on the floor,
Fallen leaves in heaps block up the door.
For she, my pride, my lovely one is lost,
And I am left, in hopeless anguish tossed.

(Herbert Giles)

Discuss these questions.

1 How is death described in this poem?

2 Which translation is more moving?
Give reasons for your choice.

B SPEAKING AND LISTENING   **READING**   **WRITING**

An early reader said that Waley's work was like looking at life on 'a new planet'. Ancient China is certainly strange but the human feelings and situations described in the poems are just like those of people today.

Here, for example, are some love stories. Read them on your own and write your answers to the questions that follow. The first is from the fourth centur

PLUCKING THE RUSHES

(a boy and a girl are sent to gather rushes for thatching)

Green rushes with red shoots,
Long leaves bending to the wind—
You and I in the same boat
Plucking rushes at the Five Lakes.
We started at dawn from the orchid-island:
We rested under the elms till noon.
You and I plucking rushes
Had not plucked a handful when night came!

By contrast, this sixth-century poem is about unhappy love.

Compare the **settings** of the two poems.

1 What stories do they tell?

2 What do the smooth **style** of the first translation, and the jagged style of the second tell you about the people in the stories?

THE EJECTED WIFE

Entering the Hall, she meets the new wife;
Leaving the gate, she runs into former husband.
Words stick; does not manage to say anything.
Presses hands together: stands hesitating.
Agitates moon-like fan, sheds pearl-like tears,
Realises she loves him as much as ever -
Present pain never come to an end.

C **SPEAKING AND LISTENING**   **READING**   WRITING

Here are some war poems. Only constant battling against enemies and rebels kept China secure.

The first was written by an army general in the first century and describes the dreadful moment of parting known to soldiers and wives throughout history. Read the poem with a partner and discuss the questions that follow.

Vocabulary

plaited: part of wedding ceremony

1 Which lines describe the couple's love for each other?

2 How exactly do they part?

3 How does the general console himself?

TO HIS WIFE

Since our hair was plaited and we became man and wife
The love between us was never broken by doubt.
So let us be merry this night together,
Feasting and playing while the good time lasts.

_____

I suddenly remember the distance that I must travel;
I spring from bed and look out to see the time.
The stars and planets are all grown dim in the sky;
Long, long is the road; I cannot stay.
I am going on service, away to the battle-ground,
And I do not know when I shall come back.
I hold your hand with only a deep sigh;
Afterwards, tears – in the days when we are parted
With all your might enjoy the spring flowers,
But do not forget the time of our love and pride.
Know that if I live, I will come back again,
And if I die, we will go on thinking of each other.

Refugees are another grim part of any war. Chen Tzu-Lung fought in a seventeenth-century war between the Ming rulers and Manchu rebels. Serving as a Ming soldier, he killed himself when captured by the enemy. His poem describes a couple fleeing from a town, threatened by Manchus, into a deserted countryside. Read the poem, and write answers to the questions that follow.

THE LITTLE CART

The little cart jolting and banging through the yellow haze
  of dusk.
  The man pushing behind: the woman pulling in front.
They have left the city and do not know where to go.
"Green, green, those elm-tree leaves: *they* will cure my
  hunger,
If only we could find some quiet place and sup on them
  together."

The wind has flattened the yellow mother-wort:
  Above it in the distance they see the walls of a house.
"*There* surely must be people living who'll give you some-
  thing to eat."
They tap at the door, but no one comes: they look in, but
  the kitchen is empty.
They stand hestitating in the lonely road and their tears fall
  like rain.

1 What particular details express the misery of the refugee's life in war?

2 Which key words show their longings and their unhappiness?

3 Look over these two war poems. What stories do they tell? How are they different and how the same in their pictures of war? Which is more moving?

Review

What do you find strange and interesting about these Chinese poems?

What are their strengths and weaknesses? Which one is the best?

Discuss together.

Homework

Read this mysterious little poem.

Write a story about this situation. Include these ideas.

● Who are the people involved?
● Where do they live?
● What has happened?
● What is the message? Why is the person (man or woman) so upset?

YELLOW DUSK

Yellow dusk: messenger fails to appear.
Restraining anger, heart sick and sad.
Turn candle towards bed-foot;
Averting face—sob in darkness.

Christmas stories

Aims

- To trace the ways in which a writer structures a poem to prepare the reader for the ending.
- To infer and deduce meanings using evidence in the poem.

Starter session

No one writes about Christmas better than Charles Dickens (1812–1870). In *Pickwick papers*, Mr. Pickwick and his friends meet at a country house for Christmas:

'This,' said Mr. Pickwick, looking round him, 'this is, indeed, comfort.'

'Our invariable custom, ' replied Mr. Wardle. 'Everybody sits down with us on Christmas Eve… and here we wait, until the clock strikes twelve, to usher Christmas in, and beguile the time with forfeits and old stories…'

Up flew the bright sparks in myriads as the logs were stirred…

Christmas is a time for story-telling. People today also enjoy stories, in print or on film, at Christmas. Note down the names of any stories or TV films you have liked recently. You may want to include the Christmas story from the Bible, too. Share your ideas with the class.

Introduction

Christmas **narrative** poems are popular. Here is a tiny story by Thomas Hardy (1840–1928). It has a powerful message behind it.

What story does this poem tell? Could there be a deeper meaning here for all of us? What words applied to the thrush could also apply to the world's poor?

THE REMINDER

While I watch the Christmas blaze
Paint the room with ruddy rays,
Something makes my vision glide
To the frosty scene outside.

There, to reach a rotting berry,
Toils a thrush – constrained to very
Dregs of food by sharp distress,
Taking such with thankfulness.

Why, O starving bird, when I
One day's joy would justify,
And put misery out of view,
Do you make me notice you?

Vocabulary

ruddy: red

constrained: forced

toils: struggles

Development

In this activity, you are going to infer and deduce meanings using evidence from a poem. In 'Christmas at sea' by Robert Louis Stevenson (1850–1894), a boy has left his home on the coast of Scotland to run away to sea. When a storm breaks out on his first voyage and the sailing ship is driven into a dangerous bay by the tide, he regrets what he has done.

FROM CHRISTMAS AT SEA

[...] All day we tacked and tacked between the South Head and the North;
    All day we hauled the frozen sheets, and got no further forth;
All day as cold as charity, in bitter pain and dread,
    For very life and nature we tacked from head to head.

We gave the South a wider berth, for there the tide-race roared;
    But every tack we made we brought the North Head close aboard:
So's we saw the cliffs and houses, and the breakers running high
    And the coastguard in his garden, with his glass against his eye.

The frost was on the village roofs as white as ocean foam;
    The good red fires were burning bright in every 'longshore home;
The windows sparkled clear, and the chimneys volleyed out;
    And I vow we sniffed the victuals as the vessel went about.

The bells upon the church were rung with a mighty jovial cheer;
    For it's just that I should tell you how (of all days in the year)
This day of our adversity was blessed Christmas morn,
    And the house above the coastguard's was the house where I was born.

O well I saw the pleasant room, the pleasant faces there,
    My mother's silver spectacles, my father's silver hair;
And well I saw the firelight, like a flight of homely elves,
    Go dancing round the china-plates that stand upon the shelves.

And well I know the talk they had, the talk that was of me,
    Of the shadow on the household and the son that went to sea;
And O the wicked fool I seemed, in every kind of way,
    To be here and hauling frozen ropes on blessed Christmas Day.

They lit the high sea-light, and the dark began to fall.
    'All hands to loose topgallant sails,' I heard the captain call.
'By the Lord, she'll never stand it,' our first mate, Jackson, cried.
    ...'It's the one way or the other, Mr Jackson,' he replied.

Vocabulary

tacked: sailed to and fro
sheets: ropes
victuals: food
adversity: difficulties

Make notes on these questions.

1 What are the horrors of life on a sailing ship in winter?

2 The coastal village looks delightfully safe from the sea. Which words and **phrases** tell you this?

> She staggered to her bearings, but the sails were new and good,
>   And the ship smelt up to windward just as though she understood.
> As the winter's day was ending, in the entry of the night
>   We cleared the weary headland, and passed below the light.
>
> And they heaved a mighty breath, every soul on board but me,
>   As they saw her nose again pointing handsome out to sea;
> But all that I could think of, in the darkness and the cold,
>   Was just that I was leaving home and my folks were growing old.

3 The boy recognises the village as his birthplace. What pictures of home and family come into his mind?

4 Most sailors are glad when the ship escapes from danger. How does this boy feel? What does he worry about in the last line?

5 **Irony** is a grim kind of joke played by fate. What ironies can you find in this narrative poem?

B

In this activity, you will trace ways in which a poem is structured to prepare the reader for the ending. The poem is the sort of Christmas tale that Pickwick might have told by the fire. Its author, Thomas Haynes Bayly (1797–1839), was a popular poet and dramatist. It's Christmas at the baron's castle. His beautiful daughter has just married Lovell, a young lord. In a break in the dancing, the girl suggests a game of hide-and-seek. Read the first part and find out what happens.

With a partner try to predict what happens next.

(Like all good stories, it has an amazing twist.) Write quick notes.

Vocabulary

blithe: happy

tarry: wait

lurking: hiding

sought: looked for

THE MISTLETOE BOUGH

> The mistletoe hung in the castle hall,
> The holly branch shone on the old oak wall;
> And the baron's retainers were blithe and gay,
> And keeping their Christmas holiday.
> The baron beheld with a father's pride
> His beautiful child, young Lovell's bride;
> While she with her bright eyes seemed to be
> The star of the goodly company.
>
> 'I'm weary of dancing now,' she cried;
> 'Here tarry a moment – I'll hide! – I'll hide!
> And, Lovell, be sure thou'rt first to trace
> The clue to my secret lurking place.'
> Away she ran – and her friends began
> Each tower to search, and each nook to scan;
> And young Lovell cried, 'Oh where dost thou hide?
> I'm lonesome without thee, my own dear bride.'
> They sought her that night! and they sought her next day!
> And they sought her in vain when a week passed away!
> In the highest – the lowest – the loneliest spot,
> Young Lovell sought wildly – but found her not.

Now continue reading.

> And years flew by, and their grief at last
> Was told as a sorrowful tale long past,
> And when Lovell appeared, the children cried,
> 'See! the old man weeps for his fairy bride.'
>
> At length an oak chest, that had long lain hid,
> Was found in the castle – they raised the lid –
> And a skeleton form lay mouldering there,
> In the bridal wreath of that lady fair!
> Oh! sad was her fate! – in sportive jest
> She hid from her lord in the old oak chest.
> It closed with a spring! and, dreadful doom,
> The bride lay clasped in her living tomb!

Discuss these questions with a partner.

1 What superstitious explanation of the bride's disappearance is invented?

2 The truth is discovered. What exactly has happened?

3 What irony can you see in the appearance of the dead woman?

Review

Which of these Christmas stories do you find most interesting? Make brief notes and share them with the class. Refer closely to details.

Homework

1 Write a contrast poem like Hardy's, based on comfort and poverty at Christmas.

2 Write the parents' story, from 'Christmas at sea'. They discuss their son in the cottage. The coastguard comes to tell them about the ship. They recognise the name…

3 Lovell narrates his memories of the 'lost bride' incident. Do not forget the 'years flew by' gap in the story.

Exiles

Aims

- To recognise how writers' language choices can enhance meaning.
- To infer and deduce meaning using evidence from poems.

Starter session

How dreadful it would be to live in exile, to be forced to leave your home country and be unable to return. With a partner, make a list of the things that you would miss most if this happened to you. Now read your points to the class.

Introduction

Exile has become all too common in the modern world. People are forced to move from their homes by the need to find work, to escape war, disaster or cruel government.

Development

A **SPEAKING AND LISTENING**   **READING**   WRITING

In this activity, you will infer and deduce meaning from a poem. William Wordsworth (1770–1850) left his native Lake District to live briefly in London. He felt pity for the poor people who had drifted from the countryside into this 'monstrous ant hill' of a city. He linked them in his mind with the wild caged thrushes placed outside shops to attract customers by their singing.

In 'Poor Susan' he put the two ideas – country girl in exile and caged bird – together. Read the poem with a partner and discuss the questions. Feed back your answers to the class.

1 Can you work out how long Susan has been in London, and what she does for a living?

2 She slips into a daydream about her Lake District home. What causes this? What does she remember of home and her life there? What does she feel about home?

3 What happens to the vision?

4 The last stanza suggests the reason that she left home. Which words tell you this?

5 The last line returns to the thrush. How exactly are girl and bird related together?

Vocabulary

reverie: daydream

Wood Street, Lothbury, Cheapside: London streets

ails: upsets

dale: valley

tripped: skipped

russet: red/brown

THE REVERIE OF POOR SUSAN

At the corner of Wood Street, when daylight appears,
Hangs a thrush that sings loud, it has sung for three
    years:
Poor Susan has passed by the spot, and has heard
In the silence of morning the song of the bird.

'Tis a note of enchantment; what ails her? She sees
A mountain ascending, a vision of trees;
Bright volumes of vapour through Lothbury glide,
And a river flows on through the vale of Cheapside.

Green pastures she views in the midst of the dale,
Down which she so often has tripped with her pail;
And a single small cottage, a nest like a dove's,
The one only dwelling on earth that she loves.

She looks, and her heart is in heaven: but they fade,
The mist and the river, the hill and the shade:
The stream will not flow, and the hill will not rise,
And the colours have all passed away from her eyes!

Poor outcast! return – to receive thee once more
The house of thy father will open its door,
And thou once again, in thy plain russet gown,
May'st hear the thrush sing from a tree of its own.

B SPEAKING AND LISTENING   **READING**   **WRITING**

In this activity you will look at how language choices enhance meaning. Thousands of Irish people were forced to emigrate in the nineteenth century, particularly because of the devastating potato famine of the 1840s but generally to seek a more prosperous way of life.

John Masefield (1878–1967) became **Poet Laureate** but his youth was spent as a seaman on sailing ships. He never lost his sympathy for ordinary working people. Here he imagines the thoughts of a young man who is about to leave his Irish village for the United States. Read the poem and write answers to the questions.

It's the night before the departure for America. There is a celebration at the rough village pub.

1 The noise of the sea-boots makes the young man uneasy. Why?

2 Which three half-lines tell us that he is anxious and sad?

3 What are the attractive things about the Irish village that he is going to miss?

FROM THE EMIGRANT

Going by Daly's shanty I heard the boys within
Dancing the Spanish hornpipe to Driscoll's violin,
I heard the sea-boots shaking the rough planks of the floor,
But I was going westward, I hadn't heart for more.

All down the windy village the noise rang in my ears,
Old sea-boots stamping, shuffling, it brought the bitter tears,
The old tune piped and quavered, the lilts came clear and strong,
But I was going westward, I couldn't join the song.

There were the grey stone houses, the night wind blowing keen,
The hill-sides pale with moonlight, the young corn springing green,
The hearth nooks lit and kindly, with dear friends good to see,
But I was going westward, and the ship waited for me.

Review

The Australian Aboriginal poet, Kath Walker (1920–1993), had a different sort of exile. The Aborigines lost their lands and sacred places to the white Australians. She sees a gum tree in a city street as a symbol of her people. Read the poem on your own.

Which key words and comparisons link the tree, the horse and the Aboriginals? Share your ideas with the class.

Homework

1 Write the full story of Susan, as told by herself. Start with her as a child at home. What will she do after her street daydream fades?

2 Imagine the young man in 'The emigrant' some time later in America. Write two sketches: one about what he sees around his new home in New York (crowds, splendid shops, huge buildings, traffic) and one about the quiet old village home in Ireland.

MUNICIPAL GUM

Gumtree in the city street,
Hard bitumen around your feet,
Rather you should be
In the cool world of leafy forest halls
And wild bird calls.
Here you seem to me
Like that poor cart-horse
Castrated, broken, a thing wronged,
Strapped and buckled, its hell prolonged,
Whose hung head and listless mien express
Its hopelessness.
Municipal gum, it is dolorous
To see you thus
Set in your black grass of bitumen –
O fellow citizen,
What have they done to us?

Home

Aims

- To identify the main points, processes and ideas in a poem.
- To recognise how poets' language choices can enhance meaning.

Starter session

George Macdonald (1824–1905), a Victorian writer, wrote one of the shortest poems in English: just two words!

As a class, discuss the following. Why can this be called a poem? Why are 'come' and 'home' such warm, inviting words? What might be the story behind this – a runaway child, a family quarrel, a mended relationship, a spell abroad?

THE SHORTEST AND SWEETEST OF SONGS

Come
Home.

Introduction

How would you define 'home'? Robert Frost (1874–1963), the American poet, wrote a **narrative poem** about an old itinerant farm worker who returns to die on the farm where he was most happy. It includes this famous definition:

Home is the place where, when you have to go there,
They have to take you in.

('Death of the hired man')

Development

Here are some more poems on the theme of 'home'.

A SPEAKING AND LISTENING   READING   WRITING

In this activity you are going to find the main points and ideas in a poem. John Walsh (1911–1972) was an English teacher and poet for young people. Here he gives us a child's view of the perfect, but ordinary, day at home. Read the poem and discuss the questions with a partner.

GOOD FRIDAY

How good to be once more in bed!
Smooth sheets, and coverlet of pink and grey!
To spread
Tired limbs and turn my thoughts upon
The things of the day!

All a long morning clear and fine
We worked, father and I, with garden hoe
And line,
To set the first seeds of the year,
Row upon row.

'No meals today!' And laughingly
Mother brought out a tray with buttered bun
And tea;
While Simpkin nosed the fence, and found
A place in the sun.

All afternoon we worked to trim
The lawns, while father joked and Mother smiled
On him.
I moved between them, almost wanting
No other child.

Quietly at tea we sat; the clear
Flames crackled up from a fire of sticks and coal;
And near
My plate the yellow fluff catkins stood
In their green bowl.

Now bed at last, with a warm drink...
Lying so curled, and hearing, as I lie,
The chink
Of cups as Mother rinses them
And puts them by;

With sounds from out-of-doors half-heard:
Voices; a starting car; the tiny cheep
Of a bird.
I do not think it will be long
Before I sleep.

1 What do the family actually do on this day at home?

2 How do they feel about each other?

3 What does 'almost wanting no other child' mean?

4 What familiar sounds of the house are heard at bedtime?

Charlotte Mew (1869–1928) was half-forgotten after her death but is now admired. Some of her poems are about country people, and she tries to imitate the local dialect. This poem is the last thoughts of an old shepherd about his home, and the landscape nearby. People in the pre-1914 countryside often stayed there all their lives. Read the poem on your own and write answers to the questions.

OLD SHEPHERD'S PRAYER

Up to the bed by the window, where I be lyin',
Comes bells and bleat of the flock wi' they two children's clack.
Over, from under the eaves there's the starlings flyin',
And down to the yard, fit to burst his chain, yapping out at Sue I do hear
                                                    young Mac.

Turning around like a falled-over sack
I can see team ploughin' in Whithy-bush field and meal carts startin'
                                        up road to Church-Town;

Saturday arternoon the men goin' back
And the women from market, trapin' home over the down.

Heavenly Master, I wud like to wake to they same green places
Where I be know'd for breakin' dogs and follerin' sheep.
And if I may not walk in th'old ways and look on th'old faces
I wud sooner sleep.

Vocabulary

clack: loud chatter
whithy: willow
trapin': trudging
breakin': training

1 What can he hear as he lies in bed?

2 What can he see as he turns over to look from the window?

3 The last **stanza** is his prayer. What does he want the after-life to be?

In this activity you will look at how language choices can enhance meaning. It can be painful when you move house. Even if your old house was inferior to the new, it has been involved in a part of your life.

This is the **theme** of 'I remember' by Thomas Hood (1799–1845). He was a writer who struggled against debt and poor health for most of his adult life. He had good reasons for looking back with nostalgia on his boyhood home in Islington. The poem mingles memories (happy) with thoughts of Hood as an adult (sad).

Read the poem and, in a small group, discuss answers to the questions.

1 What are the key ideas in each memory picture?

2 What does Hood say about his present life?

3 What comparisons does Hood use to express his nostalgia?

4 The **rhythm** is captivating. Can you work out the **rhyme scheme** and **meter** of each **stanza**?

5 Which one is the best in **style** and content?

Vocabulary

made of light: sun shines through petals

laburnum: flowering tree

Review

Which of the poems that you have read here made most impact on you? Quickly note some points about their content and language. Then put your ideas to the class.

Homework

1 Write your own piece in verse or **prose** about an ordinary day at home. Remember to use sensory details of your surroundings and make clear your feelings for people, and for pets.

2 Imagine, in a poem or short piece of prose, an old person such as the shepherd thinking back on the home (in town or country) that she/he loves.

3 What do you know about your parents' or grandparents' childhood homes? Ask about them. Write a memory poem based on one of those homes. You could start 'I remember, I remember...'

I REMEMBER, I REMEMBER

I remember, I remember,
The house where I was born,
The little window where the sun
Came peeping in at morn;
He never came a wink too soon,
Nor brought too long a day,
But now I often wish the night
Had borne my breath away!

I remember, I remember,
The roses, red and white,
The vi'lets, and the lily-cups,
Those flowers made of light!
The lilacs where the robin built,
And where my brother set
The laburnum on his birthday,—
The tree is living yet!

I remember, I remember,
Where I was used to swing,
And thought the air must rush as fresh
To swallows on the wing:
My spirit flew in feathers then,
That is so heavy now,
And summer pools could hardly cool
The fever on my brow!

I remember, I remember,
The fir trees dark and high;
I used to think their slender tops
Were close against the sky;
It was a childish ignorance,
But now 'tis little joy
To know I'm farther off from heav'n
Than when I was a boy.

Shape poems

Aims

- To recognise how poets' language choices can enhance meaning.
- To explore how form contributes to meaning in poems from different times and cultures.

Starter session

Lewis Carroll (1832–1898) taught maths at Oxford University. His 'Alice' books show how he loved to entertain children with his fantastic imagination. Nonsense verse was part of this. In *Alice's adventures in Wonderland* (1865), Carroll included a famous 'shape' or 'pattern' poem.

(The title is a **pun**: tale/tail. Fury is a dog (cur).)

1 Try writing out the poem in ordinary lines: there are four verses of three lines each – the last one is longer.

2 Do you think the shape of the poem contributes to its fierce little story? Discuss with a partner.

THE MOUSE'S TALE

'Fury said to
a mouse, That
he met in the
house, "Let
us both go
to law: I
will prose-
cute *you*. –
Come, I'll
take no de-
nial: We
must have
the trial;
For really
this morn–
ing I've
nothing
to do."
Said the
mouse to
the cur,
"Such a
trial, dear
sir, With
no jury
or judge,
would
be wast–
ing our
breath."
"I'll be
judge,
I'll be
jury,"
said
cun–
ning
old
Fury:
"I'll
try
the
whole
cause,
and
con–
demn
you to
death."

Introduction

Poets use all the resources of language to put across their ideas. This even includes the shape of the poem on the page. There are poems set out like angels' wings, falling rain, exploding rockets, coffins…

These poems are called 'pattern', 'shape' or, in recent times, 'concrete' poems.

Development

A

In this activity, you will explore how form contributes to meaning. Sometimes the shape can make a tremendous difference to the meaning of the poem. Have you ever, on holiday, seen fireflies gleaming in the darkness in their magical way? There are often two or more together. The American poet Paul Fleischman (b 1952) catches their wonder in his poem's form. Read this aloud with a partner. You will soon see that any other form would destroy the message.

FIREFLIES
(For two voices)

Light	Light
	is the ink we use
Night	Night
is our parchment	
	We're
	fireflies
fireflies	flickering
flitting	
	flashing
fireflies	
glimmering	fireflies
	gleaming
glowing	
Insect calligraphers	Insect calligraphers
practising penmanship	
	copying sentences
Six-legged scribblers	Six-legged scribblers
of vanishing messages,	
	fleeting graffiti
Fine artists in flight	Fine artists in flight
adding dabs of light	
	bright brush strokes
Signing the June nights	Signing the June nights
as if they were paintings	as if they were paintings
	We're
flickering	fireflies
fireflies	flickering
fireflies.	fireflies.

> **Vocabulary**
>
> *calligraphers*: fine handwriters

B

In this activity, you will see how form contributes to meaning and how language choices can enhance meaning. Guillaume Apollinaire (1880–1918) was a French poet, who, after serving bravely as a soldier, died in the last week of the First World War. His friends, Picasso, Braque and Matisse, were painting new kinds of picture – he tried to write new kinds of poem. He thought ordinary print was becoming dull so he created shape poems that he called 'calligrams'. Read these two examples and discuss the questions as a class.

The first was sent from the trenches to André Billy, a writer friend.

LETTER TO ANDRÉ BILLY. 9 APRIL 1915

Gunner/Driver One (front-line)
Here I am and send you greetings
No no you're not seeing things
My sector's number fifty-nine

I hear the whistle o f
the y the bird
beautiful bird of p r e ^{e} y

I see far a w $_{ay}$ 0   D
t he cathedral   H   E
                      M   A
                      Y   A   R
                      N D R E
                      B I L L Y

What do the two pictures represent? Can you work out what they say? These war poems are unusual in their contents, too. What do they leave out, and what do they include? Apollinaire said that 'poetry has the power to make everything more exciting and more fascinating'. Does he do that here?

The poem/letter starts in an ordinary way and then breaks into three word pictures. What does each represent? Think what the 'bird' might be in the trenches. Can you work out what the last picture says?

The second was sent a month later.

CALLIGRAM (15 MAY 1915)

The sky's as blue and black as ink
My eyes drown in it and sink

Darkness a shell whines over me
I write this under a willow tree

Review

Which of these shape poems is the most interesting and inventive? Are these poems of any value or are they just clever? Discuss with the class.

Homework

Compose a verse letter including shapes like Apollinaire. It might be about a holiday, a visit to town, to a theme park or the countryside. Do not forget that the words must say something worthwhile as well as fitting the image.

Ruins

Aims

- To look at a theme presented by different poets.
- To look closely at irony in these poems.

Starter session

There are many books and TV documentaries about lost cities. How many lost cities have you heard about or even visited? Offer your ideas to the class.

Introduction

Thebes was the capital of ancient Egypt in about 1600 BC. By the eighteenth and nineteenth centuries it was in ruins, but it had become a favourite destination for European travellers. The splendid ruins and statues showed something of the power of this lost civilisation.

Development

Richard Pococke was a British traveller who wrote 'A description of the East' (1743). He saw the ruins of Thebes and, in particular, he admired the great statues of the Egyptian Pharaoh, Rameses II (also called, in Greek, Ozymandias).

One of them was sitting, and was the largest in Egypt, the foot of it being ten feet and a half long. [There is] the very remarkable inscription that was on the vast colossus:

'I am the King of Kings, Ozymandias. If any should know how great I am, let him exceed the works that I have done.' This statue has been broken to pieces and carried away [...]

In 1817, two poets, Percy Bysshe Shelley (1792–1822) and Horace Smith (1799–1849), visited the British Museum in London to see the Egyptian relics from Thebes. They were particularly impressed by the huge statue of Rameses II. The two friends decided to have a poetry competition: each would write a **sonnet** about Rameses. Both borrowed ideas from Pococke's book.

A SPEAKING AND LISTENING **READING** WRITING

Smith's sonnet, with its 14 lines, divides into two sections: an **octet** (8 lines) and **sestet** (6 lines). Read Smith's sonnet with a partner. Discuss the questions that follow.

OZYMANDIAS

In Egypt's sandy silence, all alone,
　　Stands a gigantic leg, which far off throws
　　The only shadow that the desert knows.—
"I am great Ozymandias," saith the stone,
　　"The King of Kings; this mighty City shows
The wonders of my hand." – The city's gone, –
　　Nought but the leg remaining to disclose
The site of this forgotten Babylon.

We wonder, – and some hunter may express
Wonder like ours, when through the wilderness
　　Where London stood, holding the wolf in chase,
He meets some fragment huge, and stops to guess
　　What powerful but unrecorded race
　　Once dwelt in that annihilated place.

> Vocabulary
>
> *nought*: nothing
> *Babylon*: ancient city
> *annihilated*: destroyed

1 In the octet here, what is to be seen (and read) in the Egyptian desert?

2 What is **ironic** about this scene?

3 Exactly what is happening in the sestet? What further ironies are there?

4 How do the octet and sestet connect, and what is their general message about human vanity?

Now, on your own, read Shelley's sonnet, which includes his trademark hatred of any cruel, unjust ruler. Write answers to the questions.

OZYMANDIAS

I met a traveller from an antique land
Who said: 'Two vast and trunkless legs of stone
Stand in the desert...Near them, on the sand,
Half sunk, a shattered visage lies, whose frown,
And wrinkled lip, and sneer of cold command,
Tell that its sculptor well those passions read
Which yet survive, stamped on these lifeless things,
The hand that mocked them, and the heart that fed:*
And on the pedestal these words appear:
"My name is Ozymandias, king of kings:
Look on my works, ye Mighty, and despair!"
Nothing beside remains. Round the decay
Of that colossal wreck, boundless and bare
The lone and level sands stretch far away.'

*The hand that mocked them, etc.: the sculptor imitated the ugly expressions on the king's face but Ozymandias' cruel heart created them

Vocabulary

antique: ancient
trunkless: bodiless
visage: face
mocked: imitated
pedestal: statue base
mighty: other kings
colossal: huge

1 What remains of the statue survive?

2 What does the stone face tell us about the king?

3 What is the message on the statue's base?

4 What irony is expressed in the last three lines?

Review

Pococke, Smith and Shelley all quote the message on the pedestal. Who expresses it most powerfully? Give reasons for your choice.

Homework

1 Imagine that the traveller in Shelley's poem writes a letter home describing his discoveries. Include details from the Pococke extract and the two poems. Bring in the ironic comments on human power and vanity.

2 Anthony Trollope, the Victorian novelist, once wrote a story called 'The New Zealander', in which a man of the remote future explores the ruins of London. Try to write your own story or poem on this idea. Again, remember the idea of irony.

Planet Earth

Aims

- To trace the development of a theme, values and ideas in poems.
- To investigate how this theme is explored and presented.

Starter session

When the first American astronauts went to the Moon in July 1969, their photos of the lunar surface were eclipsed by those of the splendour of the planet Earth seen for the first time at a distance. A journalist wrote: 'Suddenly we are permitted to view it in context with the rest of the universe, a speck in space, a beautiful, mysterious blend of blues and browns with the white cloud its veil. Life is down there...'
What changes threaten our planet?
Make a list with a partner and then present your ideas to the class.

Introduction

Some societies revere and respect the Earth, being careful not to despoil it or take too many of its resources. A living Australian Aboriginal poet, Bill Neidjie, sums up the ideas of his people.

In the activities in this lesson you are going to look at how poets explore and present a theme.

THIS EARTH

This earth...
I never damage,
I look after.
Fire is nothing,
just clean up.
When you burn,
new grass coming up.
That mean good animal soon...
might be goose, long-neck turtle,
goanna, possum.
Burn him off...
new grass coming up,
new life all over.

Development

SPEAKING AND LISTENING   **READING   WRITING**

Air travel has allowed us to see the Earth in a new way. This is the theme of a poem by the Pakistan-born Zulfikar Ghose (b 1935). As he looks from the window of an airliner, he reflects on what he sees below. Discuss these questions with a partner.

1 As the plane climbs, Ghose sees the pattern of a city below. What conclusion does he draw?

2 At ten thousand feet, he can see a wide span of landscape. What does he now understand about the 'logic of geography'?

3 At six miles high, he can see the curvature of the Earth. What puzzles him now about human life? What is the poet saying about us and our world?

Vocabulary

inevitability: no other way of doing it

haphazard: set out at random

delineated: marked out

GEOGRAPHY LESSON

When the jet sprang into the sky,
it was clear why the city
had developed the way it had,
seeing it scaled six inches to the mile.
There seemed an inevitability
about what on ground had looked haphazard
unplanned and without style
when the jet sprang into the sky.

When the jet reached ten thousand feet,
it was clear why the country
had cities where rivers ran
and why the valleys were populated.
The logic of geography –
that land and water attracted man –
was clearly delineated
when the jet reached ten thousand feet.

When the jet rose six miles high,
it was clear that the earth was round
and that it had more sea than land.
But it was difficult to understand
that the men on the earth found
causes to hate each other, to build
walls across cities and to kill.
From that height, it was not clear why.

SPEAKING AND LISTENING   READING   WRITING

Pablo Neruda (1904–1973) was a well-known Latin-American poet. He loved to write 'elemental' poetry that appealed to ordinary people. 'Lazybones' is his answer to the American–Russian 'space race' of the 1960s. The poem asks why people need to explore space when this planet is so beautiful. Read the poem with a partner and discuss the questions.

LAZYBONES

They will continue wandering,
these things of steel among the stars,
and weary men will still go up
to brutalize the placid moon.
There, they will found their pharmacies.

In this time of the swollen grape,
the wine begins to come to life
between the sea and the mountain ranges.

In Chile now, cherries are dancing,
the dark mysterious girls are singing,
and in guitars, water is shining.

The sun is touching every door
and making wonder of the wheat.

The first wine is pink in colour,
is sweet with the sweetness of a child,
the second wine is able-bodied,
strong like the voice of a sailor,
the third wine is a topaz, is
a poppy and a fire in one.

My house has both the sea and the earth,
my woman has great eyes
the colour of wild hazelnut,
when night comes down, the sea
puts on a dress of white and green,
and later the moon in the spindrift foam
dreams like a sea-green girl.

I have no wish to change my planet.

1 In the first five lines, which words express Neruda's dislike of space exploration?

2 What are the various beauties of Chile, his homeland?
What comparisons does he use to express them?

3 Which does he like best?

4 How is the moon seen at the beginning and end of the poem?
What does the last line mean?

Review

What new ways of looking at Earth have you learned from these poems?
Which lines and ideas do you find most memorable?

Homework

1 Write a poem or prose sketch in the same style as Neruda: start with space, then move to Earth to describe the beauties of your particular home area.

2 Compose a list poem about the aspects of Earth that you love best.
Use this pattern:

I love the Earth around me:
The restless, sparkling seas with all their moods and colours;
Birdsong piercing and echoing through gardens and woodland;

Titanic

Aims

- To investigate the different ways that a theme is explored and presented by different poets.
- To identify the ways that implied and explicit meanings are conveyed in different poems.

Starter session

'The Titanic, in her pride and shame, with clocks ticking and fires burning in her luxurious rooms, plunged down to the icy depths of death!'

So wrote a journalist in April, 1912, after the liner *Titanic* sank on her first Atlantic voyage.

As a class, put together what you know about the disaster – you have probably read about it or seen the 1998 film. Then try to suggest why poets might find it an interesting subject.

Introduction

On Sunday 14 April 1912, at 11.40 p.m., the brand new passenger ship *Titanic*, crossing the North Atlantic on her way from Europe to New York, struck an iceberg. Three hours later, the huge, luxurious ship sank. Of the 2,206 people on board, only 703 were saved while 1,503 men, women and children perished, carried down in the ship herself or frozen to death in the icy water.

Development

There were so many questions. Why did a supposedly unsinkable ship go down so easily? Why were there life boats for only half the people on board? Why had ice warnings been ignored? Why did so many Third Class passengers die? But everyone agreed that most men had shown great courage by putting 'women and children first'.

In an era before TV news, the press was filled with articles, editorials, essays, letters, even sermons about the disaster. There were lots of poems, too.

A SPEAKING AND LISTENING   READING   WRITING

Harold Begbie (1871–1929) was a journalist poet, always ready to turn out sharp and quite memorable verses about great events. In this activity, you will look at how he explored the disaster. Here is part of his poem. Read it with a partner and discuss the questions.

FROM POMP AND SPLENDOUR

Pomp and splendour, pride and power
Vanished in a little hour;
Not a bubble left to show
All the skill that rusts below;
Launched the wonder of the world,
To unfathomed ruin hurled.

Yet a glory hovers there
In the bright Atlantic air,
Yet a blessing burns the wave
O'er leviathan's huge grave:
Women saw that glory flow,
Children saw that blessing glow [...]

Happy wheresoe'er they be,
Those whose bodies strew the sea,
Those who to themselves were dead
While they toiled in others' stead,
Those who waved adieu, and then
Died like Christians and like men [...]

1 How does Begbie use contrast in the description of *Titanic* in **stanza** 1?

2 What is the 'glory' hovering over the sunken ship?

3 What did the men's sacrifice prove?

Vocabulary

leviathan: huge sea monster i.e. Titanic

strew: spread out

adieu: goodbye

SPEAKING AND LISTENING   **READING**   **WRITING**

In this activity, you will identify ways in which implied and explicit meanings are conveyed in a poem. Thomas Hardy (1840–1928) wrote a poem to support the *Titanic* appeal fund. He was fascinated by the **irony** of the hugely expensive ship, full of costly possessions, lying on the sea-bed. He may have read a celebrated American sermon about the ship:

'The glassy, glaring eyes of the victims staring meaninglessly at the gilded furnishings of this sunken palace of the sea [...] jewels valued in seven figures becoming the strange playthings of the queer creatures that sport in the dark depths.'

Hardy imagines the ship resting on the sea bed. Make notes on these questions.

1 What contrasts does he offer us? (Consider the boilers, the mirrors, the jewels.)

2 What comment does he make on human vanity and 'Pride of Life'?

3 Contrast these lines with Begbie's. What does Hardy not seem to be interested in?

FROM THE CONVERGENCE OF THE TWAIN

I
In a solitude of the sea
Deep from human vanity,
And the Pride of Life that planned her, stilly couches she.

II
Steel chambers, late the pyres
Of her salamandrine fires,
Cold currents thrid, and turn to rhythmic tidal lyres.

III
Over the mirrors meant
To glass the opulent
The sea-worm crawls – grotesque, slimed, dumb, indifferent.

IV
Jewels in joy designed
To ravish the sensuous mind
Lie lightless, all their sparkles bleared and black and blind.

V
Dim moon-eyed fishes near
Gaze at the gilded gear
And query: 'What does this vaingloriousness down here?'...

Vocabulary

twain: two

she: Titanic

chambers: engine boilers

salamandrine: where a fire creature might live

thrid: threaded

lyres: musical instuments

opulent: rich

vaingloriousness: pointless display

Pride of Life: confident materialism

In this poem the contemporary Irish poet Derek Mahon (b 1941) looks at one of the people involved: Bruce Ismay, Chairman of the White Star Line that owned the *Titanic*. He saved himself in a life-boat while so many of his passengers died.

AFTER THE TITANIC

They said I got away in a boat
And humbled me at the inquiry. I tell you
I sank as far that night as any
Hero. As I sat shivering on the dark water
I turned to ice to hear my costly
Life go thundering down in a pandemonium of
Prams, pianos, sideboards, winches,
Boilers bursting and shredded ragtime. Now I hide
In a lonely house behind the sea
Where the tide leaves broken toys and hatboxes
Silently at my door. The showers of
April, flowers of May mean nothing to me, nor the
Late light of June, when my gardener
Describes to strangers how the old man stays in bed
On seaward mornings after nights of
Wind, takes his cocaine and will see no one. Then it is
I drown again with all those dim
Lost faces I never understood, my poor soul
Screams out in the starlight, heart
Breaks loose and rolls down like a stone.
Include me in your lamentations.

Vocabulary

inquiry: investigation of disaster

pandemonium: noise of falling contents of ship as she sank

ragtime: jazz tunes

cocaine: drug used to escape his guilty thoughts

lamentations: prayers of pity and sorrow

Mahon imagines the disgraced Ismay living in guilty retirement on the Irish coast. Read the poem in a small group and discuss answers to the questions.

1 How did Ismay 'sink'?

2 How did he 'freeze'?

3 Why do the broken toys and hatboxes upset him?

4 What does he think about his beautiful surroundings in his country house?

5 What does he see when he falls asleep?

6 Why did he not understand the 'lost faces'?

7 Does the poet hate or pity him? What do you think?

Review

These poems describe the disaster in different ways. Which do you find most impressive? Tell the class, supporting your points with evidence from the texts.

Homework

1 Compose a two-part poem, showing the *Titanic* and the people aboard before and after the disaster. Use details from the poems.

2 Imagine a dialogue between the gardener and a visiting reporter who wants to find out more about Ismay.

Tramp poet

Aims

- To trace the development of themes, values and ideas in a set of poems.
- To identify links between literary heritage texts and their times.

Starter session

Do you know these famous lines?

> What is this life if, full of care,
> We have no time to stand and stare?

They sound rather sentimental.
The writer, W.H. Davies (1871–1940), is known as the 'tramp poet'.
If we stopped rushing about and looked at the world, as Davies suggests,
what might we enjoy? Make a list, and then share your points with
others. Here is one of Davies' to set you thinking:

> No time to see, in broad daylight,
> Streams full of stars like skies at night.

Introduction

William Henry Davies tells his own extraordinary life story in
'Autobiography of a super-tramp' (1908). His tramping in the USA, which
involved 'jumping' trains, ended when he slipped and lost his leg beneath
the wheels. Back in London, with a wooden leg, he lived in tramps'
hostels and began to write poems. He had them printed on single sheets
and stumped around, selling them door to door. Finally he was 'discovered'
by other writers of the time, and enjoyed brief fame.

Davies loved the natural world but
wrote most forcefully about London's
poor whom he knew so well.
He felt it was shocking that so many
poor people should barely exist on
London's streets at the height of
British wealth and Imperial power.

> I see ten thousand suffering faces:
> Before me stares a wolfish eye,
> Behind me creeps a groan or sigh [...]

Development

SPEAKING AND LISTENING **READING** WRITING

In this poem, Davies contrasts the protectiveness of nature with the cruelty of city streets. Read the poem with a partner and discuss the questions.

1 Find some **adjectives** that describe the strength and grandeur of the oak.

2 You could live in this hollow oak. What comforts and pleasures does it offer?

3 What details of the lives of London's poor are given?

4 What will the tree give that is lacking in their lives?

THE OLD OAK TREE

I sit beneath your leaves, old oak,
    You mighty one of all the trees;
Within whose hollow trunk a man
    Could stable his big horse with ease.

I see your knuckles hard and strong,
    But have no fear they'll come to blows;
Your life is long, and mine is short,
    But which has known the greater woes?

Thou hast not seen starved women here,
    Or man gone mad because ill-fed –
Who stares at stones in city streets,
    Mistaking them for hunks of bread.

Thou hast not felt the shivering backs
    Of homeless children lying down
And sleeping in the cold, night air –
    Like doors and walls, in London town.

Knowing thou hast not known such shame,
    And only storms have come thy way,
Methinks I could in comfort spend
    My summer with thee, day by day.

To lie by day in thy green shade,
    And in thy hollow rest at night;
And through the open doorway see
    The stars turn over leaves of light.

Vocabulary

methinks: I think

54

In another poem, Davies looks more closely at the street people. Read it on your own and write answers to the questions.

1 Which word makes the homeless seem faceless and anonymous?

2 Why say 'flesh and soul'?

3 We like looking at the starlit sky. Why do the homeless hate it? What are they tempted to do?

4 Davies's imagination sometimes invented weird **similes**. Find an example here.

5 He ends with a description of the sounds poor people make at night. Why is 'cough like giants' so sinister?

NIGHT WANDERERS

They hear the bell of midnight toll,
And shiver in their flesh and soul;
They lie on hard, cold wood or stone,
Iron, and ache in every bone;
They hate the night: they see no eyes
Of loved ones in the starlit skies.
They see the cold, dark water near;
They dare not take long looks for fear
They'll fall like those poor birds that see
A snake's eyes staring at their tree.
Some of them laugh, half-mad; and some
All through the chilly nights are dumb;
Like poor, weak infants some converse,
And cough like giants, deep and hoarse.

C SPEAKING AND LISTENING   **READING**   WRITING

SLUM CHILDREN

Your songs at night a drunkard sings,
    Stones, sticks and rags your daily flowers;
Like fishes' lips, a bluey white,
    Such lips, poor mites, are yours.

Poor little things, so sad and solemn,
    Whose lives are passed in human crowds –
When in the water I can see
    Heaven with a flock of clouds.

Poor little mites that breathe foul air,
    Where garbage chokes the sink and drain –
Now when the hawthorn smells so sweet,
    Wet with the summer rain.

But few of ye will live for long;
    Ye are but small new islands seen,
To disappear before your lives
    Can grow and be made green.

Children were the most tragic victims of poverty. Davies contrasts his delight in the countryside with their restricted city existence. Read the poem with a partner and discuss answers to the questions.

1 What is the music that the children listen to?

2 What are their 'flowers'?

3 What are their living conditions?

4 By contrast, which lines describe the beauties of the countryside?

5 Again Davies uses strange but effective **comparisons**. Find two of them here.

Human life is degraded by poverty. The last poem is narrated by a rat, all too common in slum houses. Read the poem and write answers to the questions.

1 What are the people in the family doing as the mother lies at home dying?

2 Why can the rat attack so easily?

3 What does he intend to do? What will the family find when they return?

4 Which lines make the rat sound terrifying?

5 What is the **ambiguity** in the last line?

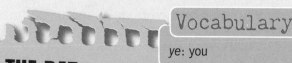

> Vocabulary
>
> ye: you

THE RAT

'That woman there is almost dead,
Her feet and hands like heavy lead;
Her cat's gone out for his delight,
He will not come again this night.

'Her husband in a pothouse drinks,
Her daughter at a soldier winks;
Her son is at his sweetest game,
Teasing the cobbler old and lame.

'Now with these teeth that powder stones,
I'll pick at one of her cheek-bones:
When husband, son and daughter come,
They'll soon see who was left at home.'

Review

Davies is an angry writer in these poems about the poor. Which of these poems made most impact on you? Make brief notes and then discuss with the class.

Homework

1 You are a social investigator studying poverty in pre-1914 London. Write a forceful report describing what you find. Use detail from the poems as your evidence.

2 Country and city: write two sketches comparing the beauties of the countryside with the horrors of Davies's city.

Lucy poems

Aims

- To trace the development of a theme or idea in a set of poems.
- To read substantial texts considering subject matter, style and technique.

Starter session

Lucy is a dream girl invented by William Wordsworth (1770–1850). He wrote a series of poems about her brief life, his love for her, and her early death.
Read one poem together.

What do you learn about Lucy – age, character, where she lived – from this restrained **elegy**?
Two **similes** describe her.
Why are they so appropriate?

She dwelt among the untrodden ways
　　Beside the springs of Dove,
A maid whom there were none to praise
　　And very few to love:

A violet by a mossy stone
　　Half hidden from the eye!
– Fair as a star, when only one
　　Is shining in the sky.

She lived unknown, and few could know
　　When Lucy ceased to be;
But she is in her grave, and, oh,
　　The difference to me!

Introduction

Wordsworth and his beloved sister Dorothy spent the winter of 1798–99 in Germany, trying to study the language. In their lodging above a draper's shop in Goslar, Wordsworth wrote some of his greatest poems, including some about Lucy.

The Lucy **sequence** outlines a relationship between 'I' (who might be Wordsworth) and a girl who suddenly dies. Was she real? She was probably invented. His poet friend Samuel Coleridge commented, 'Whether she had any reality I cannot say. Most probably he had fancied the moment in which his sister might die'.

Development

READING **WRITING**

Strange fits of passion have I known:
And I will dare to tell,
But in the Lover's ear alone,
What once to me befell.

When she I loved looked every day
Fresh as a rose in June,
I to her cottage bent my way,
Beneath an evening-moon.

Upon the moon I fixed my eye,
All over the wide lea;
With quickening pace my horse drew nigh
Those paths so dear to me.

Vocabulary

fits of passion: moods

befell: happened

lea: meadow

boon: gift

fond: foolish

wayward: wild

The 'Lucy' poems show snapshots of the relationship. Here 'I' visits Lucy's remote cottage in the evening. Read the poem and write answers to the questions.

And now we reached the orchard-plot;
And, as we climbed the hill,
The sinking moon to Lucy's cot
Came near, and nearer still.

In one of those sweet dreams I slept,
Kind Nature's gentlest boon!
And all the while my eyes I kept
On the descending moon.

My horse moved on; hoof after hoof
He raised, and never stopped:
When down behind the cottage roof,
At once, the bright moon dropped.

What fond and wayward thoughts will slide
Into a Lover's head!
'O mercy!' to myself I cried,
'If Lucy should be dead!'

1 What is the situation described in the poem?

2 How are the girl and the moon connected throughout?

3 What does the moon's sudden setting make him think about Lucy?

4 Now look back at **stanza** 1.

5 Why would only a lover understand this story?

The manuscript has one extra stanza that was not published.

I told her this; her laughter light
    Is ringing in my ears:
And when I think upon that night
    My eyes are dim with tears.

Would you have included this? Say why.

SPEAKING AND LISTENING **READING** WRITING

A second poem is about Wordsworth travelling abroad and missing Lucy.
Read it with a partner and discuss answers to the questions.

travelled among unknown men,
  In lands beyond the sea;
or, England! did I know till then
  What love I bore to thee.

Tis past, that melancholy dream!
  Nor will I quit thy shore
A second time; for still I seem
  To love thee more and more.

Among thy mountains did I feel
  The joy of my desire;
And she I cherished turned her wheel
  Beside an English fire.

Thy mornings showed, thy nights concealed
  The bowers where Lucy played;
And thine too is the last green field
  That Lucy's eyes surveyed.

1 What did 'I' do?

2 How does he now feel
   about England?

3 What is the centre of his
   love for England?

4 What picture of Lucy is
   given in the last two lines?

5 Which word does
   Wordsworth avoid in
   this poem?

Vocabulary

lands: France/Germany

wheel: spinning wheel

bowers: places in the woods

C **SPEAKING AND LISTENING** **READING** WRITING

The final poem in the sequence is considered to be the best. Coleridge
called it 'a most sublime **epitaph**'. Read it in a small group and discuss
answers to the questions.

1 What picture of Lucy is given in stanza 1?

2 What terrible change has come in
   the second?

3 Which painful events are not described
   in the space between the stanzas?

4 Why repeat 'no' and 'and' so often in
   stanza 2? Again which word is
   avoided here?

5 The usual picture of death is coffins,
   funerals, gravestones, etc. Wordsworth
   ignores these. What does he find so
   horrible about Lucy being dead in stanza 2?

A slumber did my spirit seal;
  I had no human fears:
She seemed a thing that could not feel
  The touch of earthly years.

No motion has she now, no force;
  She neither hears nor sees;
Rolled round in earth's diurnal course,
  With rocks, and stones, and trees.

Vocabulary

A slumber etc. 'I' never
worried about Lucy

diurnal: daily

Review

There is a fifth Lucy poem which connects her with the beauties of nature. What extra ideas do these lines give us? Discuss these stanzas as a class.

FROM THREE YEARS SHE GREW

[...]The stars of midnight shall be dear
To her; and she shall lean her ear
  In many a secret place
Where rivulets dance their wayward round,
And beauty born of murmuring sound
  Shall pass into her face [...].

The poem ends with Lucy's death.

[...] How soon my Lucy's race was run!
  She died and left to me
This heath, this calm and quiet scene,
The memory of what has been
  And never more shall be.

Homework

1 Compose a story about the relationship of Lucy and 'I', using details from the poems. You may wish to add your own ideas about their first meeting and the circumstances of her death.

2 Write about all four poems, outlining their contents and including comment on anything you find interesting about their form, **style** and **diction**. Quote from the poems to illustrate your points.

Adlestrop

Aims

- To identify the ways that implied and explicit meaning are conveyed in poems.
- To read a substantial poem looking closely at subject matter, style and technique.

Starter session

Read this short poem by Edward Thomas (1878–1917). He was killed in the First World War and is listed among its many fine poets. He writes indirectly about the tragedy of 1914–1918.

Think about this one-sentence poem. To what negative **phrase** does it lead? Which other suggestions of death in war can you find? What are the two opposite ideas included in this poem?

THE CHERRY TREES

The cherry trees bend over and are shedding
On the old road where all that passed are dead,
Their petals, strewing the grass as for a wedding
This early May morn when there is none to wed.

Introduction

Before the war, Thomas was a journalist, book reviewer and writer of descriptions of the old, pre-motor-car English countryside that he explored on long walking tours. It was his friend Robert Frost (1874–1963) – the American poet then living in England – who persuaded Thomas to write poems. So he began at the age of 36, composing some 140 poems before his death at the Battle of Arras in April 1917.

Development

SPEAKING AND LISTENING **READING** WRITING

'A private' is a typical poem from early 1915. Thomas enjoyed talking to countrymen on his long walks. The ploughman might therefore be a real person. Read the poem with a partner and discuss the questions.

Vocabulary

Mrs. Greenland, etc.:
under hawthorn bushes

A PRIVATE

This ploughman dead in battle slept out of doors
Many a frozen night, and merrily
Answered staid drinkers, good bedmen, and all
    bores:
'At Mrs. Greenland's Hawthorn Bush', said he,
'I slept.' None knew which bush. Above the town,
Beyond 'The Drover', a hundred spot the down
In Wiltshire. And where now at last he sleeps
More sound in France—that, too, he secret keeps.

1 How does the ploughman live?

2 What happens to him at the end of the poem?

3 What impressions do you get of his personality?

4 The apparently straightforward poem has deeper meanings.

5 The title, for example, is **ambiguous**. Why is this?

6 Thomas avoids the word 'war', giving us only 'France', where the battlefront was. Why choose a 'ploughman' as a subject? (Think of the Bible's 'swords beaten into ploughshares'.)

7 What comment, then, is Thomas making about the waste of life in war?

SPEAKING AND LISTENING **READING** WRITING

Thomas's 'Adlestrop', also written in 1915 just before he joined the army, has become one of the most popular poems of the twentieth century. On 23 June, 1914, Thomas travelled by rail to see his friend Robert Frost. The express steam train stopped, unusually, at Adlestrop station. Thomas recorded the moment in his notebook:

A glorious day [...] we stopped at Adlestrop, through the willows could be heard a chain of blackbirds' songs at 12.45 and one thrush and no man seen, only a hiss of engine letting off steam [...] banks of long grass, willowherb and meadowsweet, extraordinary silence between two periods of travel – looking out on grey stones between metals and the shining metals and over it all the elms willows and long grass – one man clears his throat – a greater than rustic silence [...] Stop only for a minute till signal is up.'

Some months later Thomas scribbled another note 'Train stopping outside Adlestrop station June 1914', and then began to write the poem. Read the poem and discuss answers to the questions in a small group.

1 Why start with 'Yes'? Thomas observes the scene closely. Which senses does he use in **stanzas** 1 and 2?

2 Full stops and line endings create heavy pauses in these stanzas. What sound quality of the place do these emphasise?

3 What does he see at the station? (Notice how his vision moves outwards.) What does he become aware of in the last stanza? What does that tell us about the pre-1914 countryside?

4 Compare the notebook entry and the poem. What has he included or added, and what left out?

5 Think hard about the poem. Is it really just about a station or a summer day? Or does it have a deeper **theme**?

ADLESTROP

Yes, I remember Adlestrop –
The name, because one afternoon
Of heat the express-train drew up there
Unwontedly. It was late June.

The steam hissed. Someone cleared his throat.
No one left and no one came
On the bare platform. What I saw
Was Adlestrop – only the name

And willows, willow-herb, and grass,
And meadowsweet, and haycocks dry,
No whit less still and lonely fair
Than the high cloudlets in the sky.

And for that minute a blackbird sang
Close by, and round him, mistier,
Farther and farther, all the birds
Of Oxfordshire and Gloucestershire.

Vocabulary

unwontedly: unusually

no whit: not a bit

Review

Thomas's poems are apparently straightforward but contain deeper meanings. Which poem impresses you most in this respect? Make brief notes and then try to explain your choice to the rest of the class.

Homework

1 Think of a place that you remember well. Note down sense detail (see, hear, touch, taste, smell) connected with this place. Now write a sketch (which might become a poem) that begins:

Yes, I remember...

2 Write about the idea of war and peace in these three Thomas poems. (Remember that 23 June 1914 was five days before the Sarajevo assassination of the Austrian Arch-duke that began the First World War.)

Lonely bride

Aims

- To recognise how a text refers to and reflects the culture in which it was produced.
- To analyse the overall structure of a text to see how ideas are developed.

Starter session

In the Western World, most of us are used to the idea of a free, personal choice of marriage partner. Some cultures prefer an arranged marriage. With a partner, list the advantages and disadvantages of each idea, and then discuss as a class.

Introduction

Rabindranath Tagore (1861–1941) was an Indian writer, as well as being a painter, educator and musician. His poems were translated from Bengali into English in 1912 and he was awarded the Nobel Prize for Literature in 1913. Although he was not a politician, he contributed generally to the movement that gave India independence in 1947. One of his songs is the Indian national anthem.

In 1890, he wrote 'Bride' about a teenage girl who leaves her country village to enter an arranged marriage in the city.

Development

A **SPEAKING AND LISTENING** **READING** WRITING

Read together the first part of this poem and discuss the questions which follow. The unfamiliar-looking but haunting broken lines – we have nothing like this in English – imitate Tagore's Bengali verse form.

The young, unhappy bride is day-dreaming at her grim new home in the city. She thinks back to her happy girlhood in a country village. The cool evening was the best time. She half hears the old cry inviting her to the pleasant evening task of fetching water.

BRIDE

'Day's ending, let us go and fetch water.'
I seem to hear from afar   that old evening call –
    But where is the shade and the water?
    Where are the steps and the fig-tree?
As I sit alone with my thoughts   I seem to hear
    'Day's ending, let's go and fetch water.'

    Pitcher at my hip, the winding path –
Nothing but fields to the left   stretching into haze,
    To the right the slanting bamboo-grove.
The evening sunlight shines   on the blackness of the pool,
    The woods round its edge are sunk in shade.
I let myself idly float   in the pool's deep calm,
    The koel on the bank has sweetness in its song.
Returning I suddenly see   above the dark trees,
    Painted on the sky, the moon.

    The wall, split by the peepul tree –
    I used to run there when I woke.
On autumn mornings the world   glistened with dew,
    Clusters of oleanders bloomed.
Two creepers covering the wall   with their flow of green
    Were laden with purple flowers.
I sat in my hiding-place   peering through cracks,
    My sari trailed on the ground.

    Field after field, and on the horizon
    A distant village blending with the sky.
Next to me ancient palm-trees   stand so densely
    Their dark-green foliage merges.
I can see the dam's thin line,   its water glinting ,
    Herd-boys crowd its edge.
The path goes out of sight,   I do not know where –
    Who knows through what new places?

What were the lovely features of the walk to the pool? Where else did she love to go and what did she find there? Why mention the path leading away from the village?

In the second part, the bride is in the city. Read it with a partner and discuss the questions.

Oh, this city with its stony body!
Its massive loveless fist   has squeezed and crushed
   A young girl's feelings, pitilessly.
Where are the boundless fields,   the open path,
   The birdsong, the trees, the shadows?

There seem to be people all around me,
   I can't speak my heart in case they hear me.
Weeping is wasted here,   it is stopped by walls,
   My weeping always comes back to me.

   No one understands why I cry,
   They wonder, they want to know the cause.
'Nothing pleases the girl,   she ought to be ashamed,
   It's always the same with girls from villages.
All these friends and relations   to keep her company,
   But she just sits in a corner and shuts her eyes!'

They point at my body or face,
   They argue about how I look –
I feel like a garland-seller   my wares examined,
   Tested for quality, coldly.

I loiter alone amidst them all,
   Each day hangs so heavily.
People here are like worms   crawling between bricks,
   There is no love, there is no gaiety.

1 There are no lovely descriptions here. The city and its effect on her are described in a powerful **metaphor**. What is this?

2 Above all, she feels shut in, as Tagore himself did in the city. Which half line defines this feeling?

3 How do other people in the new family treat her? What **simile** does she apply to herself? What does she miss most?

In the last part, she misses her mother desperately, and wonders sadly about her future. Read it on your own and write answers to the questions.

1 What memory pictures of her mother does she give us?

2 How are mother and moon connected?

3 What does the girl want to do as the moonlight enters her room? How will her new family (the 'spies') react?

4 Whom, strangely, does she not mention throughout this poem?

5 Why is 'exiled' such a sad word?

6 The old village pool and the evening call are mentioned again at the end? What new sinister force do they have there?

Vocabulary

quench: put out

What of you, mother, where are you?
You can't have forgotten me, surely?
When you sit outside on our roof   beneath the new moon
Do you still tell fairy-stories?
Or do you, alone in bed,   lie awake at night,
In tears and sickness of heart?
Take flowers to the temple at dawn to offer your prayers
For your exiled daughter's well-being?

Here also the moon rises over the roof,
Its light is at my door and begs for entry.
I feel that it wandered widely   before it found me,
It sought me because it loved me.
I forget myself for a moment,
I rush to fling open the door.
At once the spies all around me   rise like a storm,
Swoop with their cruel authority.

They won't give love, they won't give light.
I feel all the time it would be good to die,
To sink in the lap of the water of the pool,
In its shady darkness, its cool black depths.
Keep on, keep on with your evening call –
'Day's ending, let's go and fetch water.'
When will my evening come?   All playing end?
The cooling water quench all fires?
If anyone knows, tell me when.

Review

Look down the separate second-half lines. They seem to give a summary of the poem's mood and ideas.
Choose *three* that you find especially effective. Read them to the class, explaining why you find them moving.

Homework

'My old life/my new life': compose contrasting prose descriptions of the girl's life in the village with her mother, and the marriage in the city surrounded by suspicion. Invent more about her city home. Include her feelings of being trapped.

Animal encounters

Aims

- To analyse a poem to identify how key ideas are developed.
- To see how a theme is explored by poets.

Starter session

Great poets have always felt sympathy with our fellow creatures. Here is the American, Walt Whitman (1819–1892).

FROM SONG OF MYSELF

I think I could turn in and live with animals, they are so
    placid and self-contained,
I stand and look at them long and long.

They do not sweat and whine about their condition, [...]
Not one is dissatisfied, not one is demented with the mania
    of owning things,
Not one kneels to another, nor to his kind that lived
    thousands of years ago,
Not one is respectable or unhappy over the whole earth.

Vocabulary

placid: mild
demented: mad

What does he have to say about the contrast of animals and people? What are your opinions? Share your ideas with the class.

Introduction

Animals are victims. Thousands of creatures are killed on the roads each year. If we stop to consider them, pity and horror may hit us hard. This happened to the Scottish poet, Norman MacCaig (1910–1997).

INTERRUPTION TO A JOURNEY

The hare we had run over
Bounced about the road
On the springing curve
Of its spine.

Cornfields breathed in the darkness,
We were going through the darkness and
The breathing cornfields from one
Important place to another.

We broke the hare's neck
And made that place, for a moment,
The most important place there was,
Where a bowstring was cut
And a bow broken forever
That had shot itself through so many
Darknesses and cornfields.

It was left in that landscape.
It left us in another.

Development

Accidents are one thing; deliberate hunting to death another. Some argue that pest control is necessary but others believe killing for profit is detestable.

David Herbert Lawrence (1885–1930), an observer of people in his novels, plays and poems, also had an insight into the natural world. 'Mountain lion' is typical. Looking for better health, Lawrence restlessly travelled the world. In 1922, he stayed for a time in New Mexico. In January 1923, he and his wife explored the Lobo canyon near Taos.

In this activity you will analyse a poem to see how key ideas are developed. Write your answers to the questions. Read the first half of Lawrence's **free verse** poem.

MOUNTAIN LION

Climbing through the January snow, into the Lobo canyon
Dark grow the spruce trees, blue is the balsam, water sounds
    still unfrozen, and the trail is still evident.

Men!
Two men!
Men! The only animal in the world to fear!

They hesitate.
We hesitate.
They have a gun.
We have no gun.

Then we all advance, to meet.

Two Mexicans, strangers, emerging out of the dark and snow and
    inwardness of the Lobo valley.
What are they doing here on this vanishing trail?

What is he carrying?
Something yellow.
A deer?

Que tiene, amigo?
Leon —

He smiles, foolishly, as if he were caught doing wrong.
And we smile, foolishly, as if we didn't know.
He is quite gentle and dark-faced.

It is a mountain lion.
A long, long slim cat, yellow like a lioness.
Dead.

He trapped her this morning, he says, smiling foolishly.

Lift up her face,
Her round, bright face, bright as frost.
Her round, fine-fashioned head, with two dead ears;
And stripes in the brilliant frost of her face, sharp, fine dark rays,
Dark, keen, fine rays in the brilliant frost of her face.
Beautiful dead eyes.

Hermoso es!

1 Lawrence quickly describes the landscape. What does he see?

2 'Men!' is a shock line. Why might they be afraid of men in this place?

3 Why does he say 'The only animal in the world to fear'?

4 Why are both sides embarrassed as they talk?

5 Which well-chosen words and comparisons describe the lion?

6 Why have the hunters killed it?

Vocabulary

Que tiene, amigo?: what have you got there, friend?

Leon: lion

Hermoso es: it is beautiful

B *SPEAKING AND LISTENING*   *READING*   WRITING

Now read more of the poem, as the travellers continue into the mountains and find the lion's cave. Discuss the questions with a partner.

1 What are his various thoughts as he stands there looking out at the mountains?

2 How does he compare 'a million or two of humans' to one lion?

3 What, generally, is Lawrence saying about humans and wild animals in this poem?

Vocabulary

lair: home

perilous: dangerous

They go out towards the open;
We go on into the gloom of Lobo.
And above the trees I found her lair,
A hole in the blood-orange brilliant rocks that stick up, a little cave.

And bones, and twigs, and a perilous ascent.
So, she will never leap up that way again, with the yellow flash
of a mountain lion's long shoot!
And her bright-striped frost-face will never watch any more, out
of the shadow of the cave in the blood-orange rock,
Above the trees of the Lobo dark valley mouth!

Instead I look out.
And out to the dim of the desert, like a dream, never real;
To the snow of the Sangre de Cristo mountains, the ice of the
mountains of Picoris,
And near across at the opposite steep of snow, green trees
motionless standing in snow, like a Christmas toy.

And I think in this empty world there was room for me and a
mountain lion.
And I think in the world beyond, how easily we might spare a
million or two of humans
And never miss them.
Yet what a gap in the world, the missing white frost-face of that
slim yellow mountain-lion!

Review

Hunting is a very controversial issue. Quickly jot down three points for and three against hunting. Read your points to the class in a brisk mini-debate.

Homework

Imagine Lawrence writes a letter about this experience to his sister Ada in Nottingham. He includes:
- description of the setting
- the meeting with the hunters
- the dead lion.
- the visit to its lair
- his thoughts about the incident

Write the letter.

71

Angry poems

Aims

- To trace the development of themes, values and ideas in poems.
- To identify links between literary heritage texts and their times.

Starter session

What are the things that make you angry about the world in which you live? Make a list of ten things. Then share your ideas with the class.

Introduction

In the nineteenth century, with so much social injustice, there were many targets for anger. Some poets chose this as the subject of their work.

Development

A **SPEAKING AND LISTENING** **READING**

Joseph Skipsey (1832–1903) was writing his angry **lyrics** at the end of that century. The horror of coal mining was a particular **theme**. He felt that too many boys went down the 'dangerous pit' too early. Here is a poem about a boy starting work for the first time. Read the poem and discuss the questions with a partner.

1 The poem begins and ends with the parents' reactions. Why does father 'sigh' and mother 'weep'?

2 What exactly are they afraid of?

3 How, by contrast do the boy and his friends react?

4 What does the older generation know that the the younger does not?

Vocabulary

pit: mine
tidings: news
cronies: pals
counsel: advice

MOTHER WEPT

Mother wept, and father sighed;
  With delight a-glow
Cried the lad, 'To-morrow,' cried.
  To the pit I go.'

Up and down the place he sped,–
  Greeted old and young,
Far and wide the tidings spread,–
  Clapped his hands and sung.

Came his cronies some to gaze
  Wrapped in wonder; some
Free with counsel; some with praise;
  Some with envy dumb.

'May he,' many a gossip cried,
  'Be from peril kept;'
Father hid his face and sighed,
  Mother turned and wept.

Here is another poem that may help you to understand the parents' concerns. It gives a bleak picture of a miner's life.

5 What contrasts does Skipsey use to make his protest against miners' work?

THE STARS ARE TWINKLING

The stars are twinkling in the sky,
  As to the pit I go;
I think not of the sheen on high,
  But of the gloom below.

Not rest or peace, but toil and strife,
  Do there the soul enthral;
And turn the precious cup of life
  Into a cup of gall.

B SPEAKING AND LISTENING   **READING**   **WRITING**

The fate of exploited women workers was an injustice attacked by poets throughout the century.
But even at the end of the century, such women were still exploited. Annie Matheson (1853–1924), a clergyman's daughter who campaigned on social issues, wrote angrily on this theme in 1890. She contrasted her beautiful surroundings with the grim world of the London East End needle-woman. Read the poem extract and write answers to the questions.

FROM A SONG FOR WOMEN

Within a dreary narrow room
  That looks upon a noisesome street,
  Half fainting with the stifling heat
A starving girl works out her doom.
  Yet not the less in God's sweet air
  The little birds sing free of care,
  And hawthorns blossom everywhere.

Swift ceaseless toil scarce wins her bread:
  From early dawn till twilight falls,
  Shut in by four dull ugly walls,
The hours crawl round with murderous tread.
  And all the while, in some still place,
  Where intertwining boughs embrace,
  The blackbirds build, time flies apace.

With envy of the folk who die,
  Who may at last their leisure take,
  Whose longed-for sleep none roughly wake,
Tired hands the restless needle ply.

But far and wide in meadows green
The golden buttercups are seen,
And reddening sorrel nods between...

And if she be alive or dead
  That weary woman scarcely knows,
  But back and forth her needle goes
In tune with throbbing heart and head.
  Lo, where the leaning alders part,
  White-bosomed swallows, blithe of heart,
  Above still waters skim and dart.

God in heaven! shall I, who share
  That dying woman's womanhood,
  Taste all the summer's bounteous good
Burdened by her weight of care?
  The white moon-daisies star the grass,
  The lengthening shadows o'er them pass:
  The meadow pool is smooth as glass.

This is a poem of contrasting scenes: the horrible room where the poor worker sews, and the beautiful countryside where Annie lives.

1 Find some words and sentences that express the ugliness of the work-place.

2 Which are your favourite details of the country scene?

3 Matheson uses harsh words. What is suggested by 'roughly wake', 'hours crawl round', or 'scarce wins her bread'. `

Review

If Skipsey and Matheson were alive now, what would they choose to write angry poems about? Discuss together.

Homework

1 Imagine a conversation between the boy in 'Mother wept' and his parents. What would each say about his new job in the mine?

2 Make two word sketches of the contrasting lives in 'A song for women', one of the woman worker and one of Annie Matheson.
Begin each:
   Around me I see...
and continue
   All day long I...
Use details carefully chosen from the poem, but use a little invention, too.

Sonnets 1

Aims

- To analyse the structure of sonnets to see how key ideas are developed.
- To recognise the conventions of the sonnet form.

Starter session

Think about different forms of poetry, such as

elegy   lyric   narrative   ballad   haiku

Tell the class anything you remember about what these forms do and how they are written.

Introduction

The **sonnet** has always been a favourite form with poets. It was invented in Italy in the late Middle Ages. It has a particular shape and pattern but there are variations.

1 It has 14 lines.

2 It uses **pentameter rhythm**: a ten-**syllable** line, five of which are **stressed** (/) and five **unstressed** (u).

> If winter comes, can spring be far behind?
> u   /   u   /   u   /   u   /   u   /

3 It has two main **rhyme schemes**:
  a The Italian:
      an **octave** (8 lines) of two **quatrains** (4 lines each)
      a **sestet** (6 lines)

  b The English:
      three quatrains (3 x 4 lines)
      a **couplet** (2 lines)

Development

William Shakespeare (1564–1616) wrote 154 sonnets, to be enjoyed privately by friends. They were printed, probably against his wishes, in 1609. His great themes are love and time. In this sonnet, the narrator, who may or may not be Shakespeare, is older than his lover. He wants to show that this is not a problem: it could add intensity to their relationship.

SONNET 73

That time of year thou mayst in me behold
When yellow leaves, or none, or few, do hang
Upon those boughs which shake against the cold,
Bare ruined choirs where late the sweet birds sang.
In me thou seest the twilight of such day
As after sunset fadeth in the west,
Which by and by black night doth take away,
Death's second self that seals up all in rest.
In me thou seest the glowing of such fire
That on the ashes of his youth doth lie,
As on the deathbed whereon it must expire,
Consumed with that which it was nourished by.
   This thou perceiv'st, which makes thy love more strong,
   To love that well which thou must leave ere long.

Vocabulary

behold: see

choirs: church ruins

Death's second self: sleep

perceiv'st: see

leave: give up

Write answers to these questions.

1 Copy the first two lines and mark the pentameter rhythm.

2 Now work out the rhyme scheme, using A, B, etc.

3 What is the structure: is it English or Italian?

4 What three metaphors for himself does the narrator use in the three quatrains?

5 What is the message of the couplet?

Here is a Victorian sonnet about a three-year-old girl and her model globe. It is by Charles Tennyson (1808–1879), one of Alfred Tennyson's brothers, and a capable poet. This sonnet tells a story about an incident in family life. It is untidy in its rhyme scheme but like most English sonnets, it divides up into four sections. Read it and write answers to the questions.

1 Think first about Letty. Which adjective and verbs describe her and her joy in life?

2 Why was Letty given the globe?

3 What does she do with it at first?

4 What did the parents point out to her?

5 How did Letty react?

6 The world is old and scarred with human wars. Letty knows nothing of this, and looks at everything lovingly and innocently. What general message about love and war can you find in the poem? Which line expresses it best?

Vocabulary

tint: colour

prattled: chattered

isle: Britain

LETTY'S GLOBE

When Letty had scarce pass'd her third glad year,
And her young, artless words began to flow,
One day we gave the child a colour'd sphere
Of the wide earth, that she might mark and know,
By tint and outline, all its sea and land.
She patted all the world; old empires peep'd
Between her baby fingers; her soft hand
Was welcome at all frontiers. How she leap'd,
And laughed, and prattled in her world-wide bliss;
But when we turned her sweet unlearnèd eye
On our own isle, she raised a joyous cry,
'Oh! yes, I see it, Letty's home is there!'
And while she hid all England with a kiss,
Bright over Europe fell her golden hair.

Review

What metaphors and similes can you find in these sonnets? Look them over, make quick notes and discuss with the class.

Homework

1 Write about one of the poems in the unit. Include these topics: author/date/background; rhyme scheme; structure; rhythm; ideas and message; imagery (comparisons); what you find beautiful or interesting about it.

2 Try writing your own sonnet – about a child, a pet, a lovely place – or something that really interests you. Sonnets can be about anything in human life!

Metaphor

Aims

- To study the idea of extended metaphor.
- To compare its use in poems from different cultures.

Starter session

Read this tiny poem by Andrew Young (1881–1971). The Ridgeway is an ancient cattle-drovers' green road across southern England.

There is a **comparison** here. The footpath is like another road in life that we travel: that of love and marriage. Which two **phrases** make the comparison clear?

ON THE RIDGEWAY

Thinking of those who walked here long ago
On this greenway in summer and in snow
She said, 'This is the oldest road we tread,
The oldest in the world?' 'Yes, love,' I said.

Introduction

A **metaphor** is an indirect or suggested comparison. One thing, usually an **abstract idea**, is compared to something physical that we can see or touch. Metaphor is not a fancy invention. It reflects the way that our minds prefer seeing life in terms of real objects rather than as vague ideas.

An **extended metaphor** is carried on right through a whole poem.

Development

A SPEAKING AND LISTENING   **READING**   WRITING

Look at this poem by the American, Robert Frost (1874–1963). Frost walks in a wood. The path divides. Write answers to the questions.

THE ROAD NOT TAKEN

Two roads diverged in a yellow wood,
And sorry I could not travel both
And be one traveller, long I stood
And looked down one as far as I could
To where it bent in the undergrowth.

Then took the other as just as fair,
And having perhaps the better claim,
Because it was grassy and wanted wear;
Though as for that the passing there
Had worn them really about the same,

And both that morning equally lay
In leaves no step had trodden black.
Oh, I kept the first for another day!
Yet knowing how way leads on to way,
I doubted if I should ever come back.

I shall be telling this with a sigh
Somewhere ages and ages hence:
Two roads diverged in a wood, and I –
I took the one less travelled by,
And that has made all the difference.

Vocabulary

diverged: split apart

wanted wear: was little used

1 Is there any difference between the paths?

2 Which one does he choose and why?

3 What does he want to do about the path he has not chosen?

The last, strongly-felt line makes us think that the poem is not just about choosing foot-paths but is, more widely, about the choices we make in life. In 1912, Frost gave up a secure life as a New Hampshire farmer and teacher, and made a risky move to England to become a full-time poet.

4 How do the details of the poem fit that choice?

5 How does Frost's choice explain the force behind the last line?

Of course, 'I' could be anyone, and the two paths any of the choices we make in life.

6 What major choices will you have to make in your own life?

Now read this translated poem by the modern Russian poet, Andrei Voznesensky (b 1933). Remember, as you read, that the Russian winter can be brutally cold! Discuss the questions with a partner.

FIRST FROST

A girl is freezing in a telephone booth,
huddled in her flimsy coat,
her face stained by tears
and smeared with lipstick.

She breathes on her thin little fingers.
Fingers like ice. Glass beads in her ears.

She has to beat her way back alone
down the icy street.

First frost. A beginning of losses,
the first frost of telephone phrases.

It is the start of winter glittering on her chee
the first frost of having been hurt.

1 How old is the girl? Describe her appearance.

2 Why is she in the telephone booth and whom is she calling?

3 What is happening to her?

4 Which words make us pity her?

5 What does 'a beginning of losses' mean?

6 What are the two meanings of 'the start of winter glittering on her cheek'?

7 Now trace the extended metaphor of 'cold', 'ice' and 'frost' through the poem. You can see it best in lines 8 and 12. Do you think it is appropriate and expressive?

Review

Discuss these questions as a class.

● What is the point of using extended metaphors in these three poems?
● Which metaphor is the most interesting and convincing?

Homework

Write a story about the girl in 'First frost' and her situation. Fill in more background (home; parents; nature of the man involved) and details of her sad relationship. End with the scene where she leaves the telephone box.

Sonnets 2

Aims

- To compare ideas, values and emotions in two sonnets.
- To compare their themes and styles.

Starter session

Revise what you already know about **sonnets**.

What are the differences between the English (Shakespearean) and Italian sonnet forms?

What do these terms mean?

quatrain   octet   sestet   couplet

What is a **pentameter rhythm**?

Introduction

You have already looked at some sonnets earlier in this book (page 75).

The sonnet is a favourite form with poets writing in English. Each generation of poets wants to use the challenging form in its own way. Sonnets can be about any of the things that concern human beings: love, death, God, power, time and change, children, nature, war...

Dante Gabriel Rossetti (1828–1882) once wrote a sonnet about writing sonnets. The little poem, he said, is like a coin, with the author on one side and his subject – most probably love, life, or death – on the other. It may also record a particular experience in someone's life:

> A sonnet is a moment's monument.

If it is a happy moment, it is carved in ivory; if it is grim, it is in black ebony.

Development

A CHURCH ROMANCE

She turned in the high pew, until her sight
Swept the west gallery, and caught its row
Of music-men with viol, book and bow
Against the sinking sad tower-window light.
She turned again; and in her pride's despite
One strenuous viol's inspirer seemed to throw
A message from his string to her below,
Which said: 'I claim thee as my own forthright!'

Thus their hearts' bond began, in due time signed.
And long years thence, when Age had scared Romance,
At some old attitude of his or glance
That gallery-scene would break upon her mind,
With him as minstrel, ardent, young, and trim,
Bowing 'New Sabbath' or 'Mount Ephraim'.

Now compare two sonnets from the nineteenth century. Read 'A church romance' by Thomas Hardy (1840–1928). Hardy's father was a Dorset village stonemason in the 1830s. He also played the violin in the local church orchestra. His future wife saw him playing in the church gallery, a slightly odd figure in a 'blue swallow-tailed coat…a red and black flowered waistcoat…and French-blue trousers'. But he was good-looking and she was attracted to him.

Vocabulary

viol : violin

ardent: burning with love

New Sabbath, etc: hymns

William Wordsworth (1770–1850), the poet of the Lake District, married Mary Hutchinson in 1802. Among their several children was Catharine,

' who fills the air
With gladness and involuntary songs.'

When she died suddenly, aged 3, in June 1812, Wordsworth was devastated. He wrote a sonnet in her memory. Read it with a partner.

SURPRISED BY JOY

Surprised by joy—impatient as the wind
    I turned to share the transport—Oh! with whom
    But thee, deep buried in the silent tomb,
That spot which no vicissitude can find?
Love, faithful love, recalled thee to my mind—
    But how could I forget thee? Through what power,
    Even for the least division of an hour,
Have I been so beguiled as to be blind
To my most grievous loss!—That thought's return
    Was the worst pang that sorrow ever bore,
Save one, one only, when I stood forlorn,
    Knowing my heart's best treasure was no more;
That neither present time, nor years unborn
    Could to my sight that heavenly face restore.

Vocabulary

transport: strong feeling of joy

vicissitude: life's ups and downs

beguiled: tricked

Look at the 'story' of 'A Church Romance'.

  1 Why does 'she' find it hard to see 'him' in the gallery?

  2 She turns back but receives a sound message from him. How is this done and what is the message?

  3 What is 'their hearts' bond...in due time signed'?

  4 Time passes. Why does 'Age scare Romance'? However, even when the couple become old, some things remind her of that first meeting. What are these?

  5 Now look at the form of the sonnet.On paper, mark the pentameter rhythm of the first two lines.
     (u = unstressed syllable; / = stressed syllable).

  6 Work out the **rhyme scheme**. Is this an Italian or English sonnet?

Now, with a partner trace the rhyme scheme in 'Surprised by Joy'.
There are two quatrains and a sestet. Discuss these questions.

  7 In the first quatrain, Wordsworth turns to share a joke with Catharine. What happens then?

  8 Of what does he reproach himself in the second quatrain?

  9 What does he tell us about his feelings for Catharine in the sestet?

  10 Which words and **phrases** describe Catharine?

  11 Which lines express the horrors of death?

  12 How does the punctuation create the idea of someone thinking and changing moods rapidly?

Review

As a class, consider the two sonnets in relation to Rossetti's ideas noted in the introduction. How are they each 'a moment's monument'? Are they 'ivory' or 'ebony'? Which is more memorable? Give evidence to support your view.

Homework

1 Imagine that Hardy's mother kept a diary when she was a young woman. Write her entry about the important moment in 'A Church Romance'.

2 Compose a letter from Wordsworth to his brother John describing the incident in 'Surprised by Joy'.

3 The poets write about great themes: love and death. Compare and contrast how they see them in fresh and original ways. How do they use the sonnet form in different ways to express their ideas?

Dulce et decorum est

Aims

- To compare the ideas and values of related poems.
- To consider the language and imagery of these poems.

Starter session

In one of his poems, the Roman writer Horace saw soldiering for the Republic as a glorious duty for young men. He concluded in Latin:

> 'Dulce et decorum est pro patria mori'
> (It is sweet and fitting to die for your country.)

What was it about the nature of fighting in Roman times that allowed Horace to make this statement? Discuss briefly.

Introduction

Many people studied Latin at school in the nineteenth century. Horace's words, 'Dulce et decorum est', seemed to apply to British soldiers fighting and dying for the British Empire. Poems written during the Boer War (1899–1902) often used the motto as a title.

The battlefields of the First World War (1914–1918) produced mass slaughter. In a single attack, thousands of men might be killed. A journalist at the Battle of the Marne (1914) described 'A terrible spectacle [...] Hundreds and hundreds of bodies lie on the ground as far as the eye can reach. They are like grass cut by a scythe [...]' To avoid this hideous truth and to console relatives, civilian poets kept up the idea that war was glorious and that it was 'sweet and fitting' to die in battle.

Development

Geraldine Robertson Glasgow was one such civilian poet. In *Punch* magazine in 1916, she published this poem. Read it and discuss the questions in a small group.

FROM DULCE ET DECORUM

All life was sweet —veiled mystery in its smile;
    High in your hands you held the brimming cup;
Love waited at your bidding for a while,
    Not yet the time to take its challenge up;
Across the sunshine came no faintest breath
To whisper of the tragedy of death.

And then, beneath the soft and shining blue,
    Faintly you heard the drum's insistent beat;
The echo of its urgent note you knew,
    The shaken earth that told of marching feet;
With quickened breath you heard your country's call,
And from your hands you let the goblet fall.

You snatched the sword, and answered as you went,
    For fear your eager feet should be outrun,
And with the flame of your bright youth unspent
    Went shouting up the pathway to the sun.
O valiant dead, take comfort where you lie.
So sweet to live? Magnificent to die!

Vocabulary
cup: of life
goblet: decorated cup
valiant: brave

(Glasgow takes her ideas of the cup and the sword from Victorian paintings where life is often seen as medieval stories of heroic knights. The summer of 1914 was famously fine but the details – 'sunshine', 'soft and shining blue' – are also part of the glorious youth of the soldier.)

1 How is life described in the first **stanza**?

2 What will the young man miss by dying in battle?

3 How is the declaration of war depicted in the second stanza? How does the young man respond?

4 What **metaphor** is used to describe his joining the army?

5 Why is it 'magnificent' to die?

6 Why is this poem an unrealistic picture of modern war?

DULCE ET DECORUM EST

Bent double, like old beggars under sacks,
Knock-kneed, coughing like hags, we cursed through
    sludge,
Till on the haunting flares we turned our backs
And towards our distant rest began to trudge.
Men marched asleep. Many had lost their boots
But limped on, blood-shod. All went lame; all blind;
Drunk with fatigue; deaf even to the hoots
Of tired, outstripped Five-Nines that dropped behind.

Gas! GAS! Quick, boys! – An ecstasy of fumbling,
Fitting the clumsy helmets just in time;
But someone still was yelling out and stumbling,
And flound'ring like a man in fire or lime...
Dim, through the misty panes and thick green light,
As under a green sea, I saw him drowning.

In all my dreams, before my helpless sight,
He plunges at me, guttering, choking, drowning.

If in some smothering dreams you too could pace
Behind the wagon that we flung him in,
And watch the white eyes writhing in his face,
His hanging face, like a devil's sick of sin;
If you could hear, at every jolt, the blood
Come gargling from the froth-corrupted lungs,
Obscene as cancer, bitter as the cud
Of vile, incurable sores on innocent tongues, –
My friend, you would not tell with such high zest
To children ardent for some desperate glory,
The old Lie: Dulce et decorum est
Pro patria mori.

Wilfred Owen (1895–1918) was perhaps the greatest of the many First World War poets. He went to the Front in early 1917. In letters home he recorded the terrible things he had seen: soldiers frozen to death; a sentry blinded; No Man's Land 'crawling and wormy' with dead and wounded after an attack. Worst of all was poison gas, which attacked eyes and lungs, destroying its victims slowly and painfully.

Recovering from battle stress at a shell-shock-hospital in Edinburgh in October, 1917, Owen wrote his fiercest anti-war poem, 'Dulce et decorum est'. The first draft is addressed to what he considered contemptible civilian poets who supported war. Glasgow may have been one of them: he certainly read (and disliked) *Punch*. Read the poem and write answers to the questions.

Vocabulary

Five-Nines:	shells
guttering:	going out like a candle flame
ardent:	burning

First consider the story of the poem.

1 What are the soldiers doing and what danger suddenly threatens them?

2 How do they escape this?

3 What happens to one unlucky man? What do they do with this man as he dies slowly?

Now think about the **style**.

4 Pick out the ugly **diction** and **imagery** describing the soldiers in the first part of the poem.

5 How is the gas seen in the second part?

6 Which ugly words and **comparisons** describe the gas victim in the last part?

7 Lastly, reflect on the poem's message. 'My friend' is someone like Glasgow. What exactly does Owen say to her in the last part of the poem?

Review

Look back at Owen's poem. He uses words as weapons to attack the Latin motto. How *exactly* does he destroy the ideas of 'sweet' and 'fitting'? Suggest particular words and lines in a brief discussion.

Homework

1 Compare the two poems in this unit:
   – the pictures of soldiers in war
   – the ideas of death in battle
   – the imagery and diction of the poets.

2 Compose a **dialogue** between Owen and Glasgow. Each is determined to show the other what 'Dulce et decorum est' really means.

3 Write the story of the gas attack and its victim as told by one of his comrades.

Elegy

Aims

- To look at the idea of elegy in poems from different times.
- To compare the styles and techniques of these poems.

Starter session

An **elegy** (adjective: **elegiac**) is a poem of sadness and mourning. We all learned more about elegy when Princess Diana was killed in a car crash in 1997. Poetic words, like those of Elton John's song, summed up what many people felt.

What would you include in an elegy for Diana, or for another person who died young? Make notes and then offer your ideas to the class.

Introduction

Read this 1806 elegy by Walter Savage Landor (1775–1864). At 22, Landor had fallen in love with the beautiful 17-year-old Rose. Three years later she died in India. Landor wrote the poem quickly but it has haunted readers ever since.

Vocabulary

what avails: what is the
sceptred race: noble fa
form divine: beauty
consecrate: devote

ROSE AYLMER

Ah, what avails the sceptred race!
　　Ah, what the form divine!
What every virtue, every grace!
　　Rose Aylmer, all were thine.

Rose Aylmer, whom these wakeful eyes
　　May weep, but never see,
A night of memories and of sighs
　　I consecrate to thee.

Rose's fine qualities are wasted in death. What were they? In the first draft, Landor wrote 'For Aylmer, all were thine' and 'Sweet Aylmer'. In the final draft there are three 'Rose Aylmers'. Why is this better? Why is the name so magical? What is **ironic** about the ideas of 'eyes' in **stanza** 2?

Development

Now compare two other elegies from different centuries.

'In Memoriam' by Alfred Tennyson (1809–1892) is the longest elegy in English. It consists of 132 separate poems devoted to the memory of Arthur Hallam, Tennyson's friend, who was engaged to his sister Emily. Hallam died suddenly in 1833 and Tennyson at once started his elegies, not finishing until 1850.

Number 7 is, perhaps, one of the best. Tennyson goes to the Hallam family home in Wimpole Street, London, but his friend is no longer there. Tennyson gets right away from the usual ideas of death: graves, funerals, dark clothes... Instead death is like a shut up house that you can no longer enter. Read the poem and write answers to the questions.

FROM IN MEMORIAM

Dark house, by which once more I stand
    Here in the long unlovely street,
    Doors, where my heart was used to beat
So quickly, waiting for a hand,

A hand that can be clasped no more—
    Behold me, for I cannot sleep,
    And like a guilty thing I creep
At earliest morning to the door.

He is not here; but far away
    The noise of life begins again,
    And ghastly thrugh the drizzling rain
On the bald street breaks the blank day.

LONG DISTANCE

Though my mother was already two years dead
Dad kept her slippers warming by the gas,
put hot water bottles her side of the bed
and still went to renew her transport pass.

You couldn't just drop in. You had to phone.
He'd put you off an hour to give him time
to clear away her things and look alone
as though his still raw love were such a crime.

He couldn't risk my blight of disbelief
though sure that very soon he'd hear her key
scrape in the rusted lock and end his grief.
He *knew* she'd just popped out to get the tea.

I believe life ends with death, and that is all.
You haven't both gone shopping; just the same,
in my new black leather phone book there's your name
and the disconnected number I still call.

Vocabulary

blight: unpleasant influence

Tony Harrison (b 1930) is an outstanding contemporary poet. He often writes about his working-class childhood in Leeds. In 'Long distance', he writes an elegy for his father, who never got used to being a widower. Read the poem and discuss the questions in a small group.

'In Memoriam'

1 Why is 'dark' such a powerful word?

2 Why mention the 'hand' twice?

3 How does Tennyson behave strangely in his grief?

4 Which words tell you that he finds everyday life ugly and pointless now?

'Long Distance'

5 What various things did his father do to pretend that his wife was still alive?

6 How did he behave when his son came to visit?

7 What did the father fear his son might say?

8 The beginning of the last stanza tells us that the son thinks he is different but how does he imitate his father?

9 What do you learn about 'raw love' in this poem?

10 How is the title **ambiguous**?

11 Do you like the **colloquial style**? Where is it most vivid?

Review

Elegies are not morbid. They help us to appreciate a person's life. Which of these elegies is most moving? Read them again, and suggest your ideas to the class.

Homework

1 Write a comparison of the three elegies included in this unit:
   – What is each poem about?
   – How does the diction and form contribute to the power of the poems?
   – How do the poems compare in style and outlook?

2 Write an elegy, as a poem or in prose, to a well-loved person, in your life, or in the world at large.

3 The two poets see death as a house that is locked against you ar a phone call that cannot get through. Write notes on these questions. Which do you find more striking and appropriate? Look at the tone and language of the poems. Tennyson uses a grim simplicity and Harrison a bleakly humerous colloquial style. Which is more effective? Look closely at words and phrases.

Holocaust

Aims

- To look at authors' perspectives in texts from different cultures.
- To consider how cultural traditions have influenced these poems.

Starter session

The darkest episode of the twentieth century, the Holocaust (the mass killing of six million Jews by the German Nazis) reached its dreadful climax in 1942–1945. The names of the concentration camps – especially Auschwitz in Poland – where the killing was carried on still evoke absolute horror.

Here are some lines from a Holocaust poem by Hilda Schiff entitled 'The German Frontier':

> The black-clad figures, the brutal voices,
> The crowded cattle-trucks, the reeking odour,
> The sweat, the stench, the gas, the horror.

Remind yourself of what you already know of the Holocaust by discussing the details here in pairs. Who are the 'black-clad figures'? What are the 'cattle-trucks'? What is the 'gas'? And what is the 'horror'?

Introduction

Jews had been persecuted for centuries in Europe. The rise of Adolf Hitler and his Nazi party in Germany in the 1920s and 1930s gave this anti-Semitism new strength. The killing of Jews began when Hitler invaded Poland and Russia after 1939. A sinister Nazi conference of January 1942 proposed a 'Final Solution', the destruction of all Europe's Jews. Victims were to be gathered into concentration camps in Poland where they would be gassed to death and their bodies burned in crematoria.

Development

How can you write poems about such a huge tragedy? Grim sarcasm is one way. Ephim Fogel (b 1920), a writer and scholar, uses a dark Jewish humour to pretend to see the slaughter through the eyes of a Nazi bureaucrat like Adolf Eichmann, who administered the hideous process. Read the poem and discuss the questions with a partner.

SHIPMENT TO MAIDANEK

Arrived from scattered cities, several lands,
intact from sea land, mountain land, and plain,
Item: six surgeons, slightly mangled hands,
Item: three poets, hopelessly insane,

Item: a Russian mother and her child,
the former with five gold teeth and usable shoes,
the latter with seven dresses, peasant-styled.

Item: another hundred thousand Jews.

Item: a crippled Czech with a handmade crutch.
Item: a Spaniard with a subversive laugh;
seventeen dozen Danes, nine gross of Dutch.

Total: precisely a million and a half.

They are sorted and marked – the method is up to you.
The books must be balanced, the disposition stated.
Take care that all accounts are neat and true.

Make sure that they are all thoroughly cremated.

Vocabulary

Maidanek: concentration camp

gold teeth, etc.: anything of value was reclaimed from the bodies

Item: a word used in business invoices

subversive: anti-authority

1 The poem mixes huge numbers, which are difficult to grasp, with individuals like the poets or the Russian mother. Which are most memorable?

2 Look closely at the details. Why mention 'slightly mangled hands', 'gold teeth, 'seven dresses', 'subversive laugh'?

3 What does 'the method is up to you' mean?

4 How does Fogel use contrast in this poem?

The Polish poet, Tadeusz Rosewicz (b 1921) witnessed the German occupation of Poland, and aimed to write poems 'For the horror-stricken. For those abandoned to butchery. For survivors'.

On a visit to the grim Holocaust museum set up after the war at Auschwitz, the preserved mounds of human hair cut from prisoners to be used, supposedly, in German war industry made a huge impression on him. Read the poem and write answers to the questions.

PIGTAIL

When all the women in the transport
had their heads shaved
four workmen with brooms made of birch twigs
swept up
and gathered up the hair

Behind clean glass
the stiff hair lies
of those suffocated in gas chambers
there are pins and side combs
in this hair

The hair is not shot through with light
is not parted by the breeze
is not touched by any hand
or rain or lips

In huge chests
clouds of dry hair
of those suffocated
and a faded plait
a pigtail with a ribbon
pulled at school
by naughty boys.

Vocabulary

transport: trainload of Jews

glass: case in museum

suffocated: gassed

1 Which details of the hair are particularly horrific?

2 How do we like to think of human hair?

3 Why does the pigtail make such a strong impression on the poet?

After the war, some Nazis were brought to justice. William Heyen (b 1940), an American poet of German ancestry, wonders just how many people in Nazi Germany helped to make and sustain the Holocaust. Most survivors of that time deny knowledge of it. Read the poem with a partner and discuss the questions.

Vocabulary

Belsen/Dachau: concentration camps;

lampshade: made from human skin;

Speer: important Nazi who survived war;

pellets: of poison gas

RIDDLE

From Belsen a crate of gold teeth,
from Dachau a mountain of shoes,
from Auschwitz a skin lampshade.
Who killed the Jews?

Not I, cries the typist,
Not I, cries the engineer,
Not I, cries Adolf Eichmann,
Not I, cries Albert Speer.

My friend Fritz Nova lost his father –
a petty official had to choose.
My friend Lou Abrahms lost his brother.
Who killed the Jews?

David Nova swallowed gas,
Hyman Abrahms was beaten and starved.
Some men signed their papers,
and some stood guard,

and some herded them in,
and some dropped the pellets,
and some spread the ashes,
and some hosed the walls,

and some planted the wheat,
ans some poured the steel,
and some cleared the rails,
and some raised the cattle.

Some smelled the smoke,
some just heard the news.
Were they Germans? Were they Nazis?
Were they human? Who killed the Jews?

The stars will remember the gold,
the sun will remember the shoes,
the moon will remember the skin.
But who killed the Jews?

1 Look at **stanza** 1. What evidence survives of the Holocaust?

2 How would the typist and the engineer have contributed?

3 Why mention named Jewish victims?

4 The 'some' list grows more general as it goes on. What is the difference between the first and the last on this list?

5 Are they all equally guilty?

6 How, fancifully, does the poet think the Holocaust might be remembered in nature?

Review

Read over the poems an this section. Which do you think gives greatest insight into the Holocaust tragedy? Find some particular evidence to include in your judgement. Then discuss with the class.

Homework

Try to compose your own Holocaust poem, perhaps inspired by photographs or films you have seen, or by the British Library's haunting 'Holocaust voices' website or the Imperial War Museum's special exhibition.

Perhaps it is easier to write about one victim – Anne Frank or someone seen in a picture – than about millions.

THE HOLOCAUST EXHIBITION

Under the cover of the Second World War, for the first time in history, industrial methods were used for the mass extermination of a whole people.
The Imperial War Museum's Holocaust Exhibition uses historical material to tell the story of the Nazis' persecution of the Jews and other groups before and during the Second World War.

The Holocaust Museum is situated within the Imperial War Museum London. Entrance is free. To find out how to get here, see Planning your visit.

HOME

persecution – – education
evidence – – publications
witnesses – – links
visitors comments – articles
related events – join our mailing list

In the trenches

Aims

- To compare ideas and emotions in related poems.
- To discuss the language and imagery of these poems.

Starter session

Read this poem about the Ypres sector of the Western Front in the First World War. The poet, Herbert Asquith (1881–1947), son of the British Prime Minister, was wounded in battle.

NIGHTFALL

Sanctuary Wood, 1917

Hooded in angry mist, the sun goes down:
Steel-gray the clouds roll out across the sea:
Is this a Kingdom? Then give Death the crown,
For here no emperor hath won, save He.

This **epigrammatic** poem gives you the basic 1914–1918 situation: huge armies facing each other in trench lines that neither side can break.

The armies of two Emperors (the British King and the German Kaiser) struggle in the muddy battle-grounds near Ypres. What third Emperor is actually doing well out of the fighting?

What do these words add to this picture of war?

> hooded   angry   goes down   steel-grey

Introduction

The Western Front of 1914–1918 was a nightmare stalemate. It was, noted a 'Times' reporter in November 1914, 'a wall of men which reaches from the North Sea to Switzerland... Trenches and always trenches...and nothing showing above the surface of the ground. Day after day the butchery of the unknown by the unseen.' Civilians understood little of the conditions. Soldiers told them something in letters home but left out the worst horrors.

Development

SPEAKING AND LISTENING   READING   WRITING

Soldiers also wrote poems in which they were less restrained. Theodore Wilson (1889–1918) was a schoolmaster who had volunteered for the army. He was killed in March 1918. Here is part of his 1916 letter describing the Front:

You look over the top or through a periscope, and then you see barbed wire and more barbed wire – German wire this time, and the German line, which is being watched all day by eyes which hardly wink. The slightest movement on it is met with fire. The same goes on of course with our line. Look over the top for longer than two seconds and you're lucky to step down without a bullet through your brain [...] You hear a sound like a circular saw [...] It ends in a terrific burst – a shower of earth or bricks or metal – and sometimes a torn man to be put out of sight [...]

Privately, Wilson saw the war as 'indescribably disgusting...a great dirty tragedy'. Here is part of one of his protest poems. Read it with a partner and discuss the questions.

FROM FRANCE, 1917

[...] The bodies of men lay down in the dark of the earth:
Young flesh, through which life shines a friendly flame,
Was crumbled green in the fingers of decay...
Among the last year's oats and thistles lay
A forgotten boy, who hid as though in shame
A face that the rats had eaten...Thistle seeds
Danced daintily above the rebel weeds.

[continued over page]

Old wire crept through the grass there like a snake,
Orange-red in the sunlight, cruel as lust.
And a dead hand groped up blindly from the mould...
A dandelion flamed through ribs - like a heart of gold,
And a stink of rotten flesh came up from the dust...
With a twinkle of little wings against the sun
A lark praised God for all that he had done.

There was nothing here that moved but a lonely bird,
And the wind over the grass. Men lived in mud;
Slept as their dead must sleep, walled in with clay,
Yet staring out across the unpitying day,
Staring hard-eyed like hawks that hope for blood.
The still land was a witch who held her breath,
And with a lidless eye kept watch for death...

Vocabulary

wire: barbed wire

ribs: soldier's skeleton

1 What do you find most memorable in this picture of the trenches?

2 Find some of the **similes** and **metaphors** he uses. What is compared to what in these?

3 How does Wilson use contrast?

4 Compare the poem extract and the letter. Why is the poem so much more expressive?

B **SPEAKING AND LISTENING**   **READING**   WRITING

Siegfried Sassoon (1886–1967) was famous for his courage and his war poems, which he described as 'trench rockets sent up to illuminate the gloom'. He also kept a war diary. Here he records a dawn offensive during the Battle of Arras in April 1917.

'The 19th Brigade attacked at 5.30 a.m. I looked across at the hill where a round sun was coming up. The hill was deeply shadowed and grey-blue, and all the country was full of shell-flashes and drifting smoke. A battle picture'.

Later he turned this note into a poem. Read it and discuss the questions in a small group.

ATTACK

At dawn the ridge emerges massed and dun
In wild purple of the glow'ring sun,
Smouldering through spouts of drifting smoke that shroud
The menacing scarred slope; and, one by one,
Tanks creep and topple forward to the wire.
The barrage roars and lifts. Then clumsily bowed
With bombs and guns and shovels and battle-gear,
Men jostle and climb to meet the bristling fire.
Lines of grey, muttering faces, masked with fear,
They leave their trenches, going over the top,
While time ticks blank and busy on their wrists,
And hope, with furtive eyes and grappling fists,
Flounders in mud. O Jesus, make it stop!

1 Which words and phrases in the first sentence express the violence and danger of the attack?

2 How do the men look and behave as they advance?

3 Why is the line 'Time ticks blank and busy' so effective?

4 What has 'hope' turned into?

5 The last line shows a favourite Sassoon device: a soldier's swear-word (Jesus!) that can also be seen as a prayer. What is he praying for?

Review

Thousands of poems were written about the First World War. Hardly any are published about contemporary wars. Why is this? What other media now give us insight into the horrors of war?

Homework

1 Compare Wilson's 'France, 1917' with Sassoon's 'Attack' as pictures of trench warfare.
  Consider:
  – the scenes pictured in the poems
  – the **diction** used
  – the **imagery** involved
  – the feelings each poet has for the soldiers.
  Which is better?

2 Write your own trench poem or prose sketch. Use details given in this Unit, or from other book or film resources you may have discovered.

Memory of places

Aims

- To compare ideas, values and emotions in related poems.
- To compare themes and styles of poets from different times and cultures.

Starter session

Places can be very important in our lives. Houses, streets, pieces of countryside where we have been happy or unhappy stay in our memories. Think of such places. If you can, share some of them with the class.

Introduction

Pathetic fallacy connects our feelings with the places around us. If we are happy, the bleakest pace can seem wonderful; if we are sad or upset, the most beautiful place can seem grim. A little poem by Amy Levy (1861–1889) is an illustration. Normally she would enjoy the lovely scene. Now it seems only to mirror her distress.

IN SEPTEMBER

The sky is silver-grey; the long
  Slow waves caress the shore.–
On such a day as this I have been glad,
  Who shall be glad no more.

Development

A *SPEAKING AND LISTENING*   *READING*   WRITING

Thomas Love Peacock (1785–1866) is best remembered as a novelist, but he also wrote poems. 'Newark Abbey' was written in 1860, when Peacock was 75. It recalls the summer of 1807 when, at 22, he had courted 18-year-old Fanny Falkner.

They met at the ruins of Newark Abbey near Chertsey where Peacock lived. The engagement was broken by an interfering relative. Fanny married another but died soon afterwards. Peacock married, too. But his first love remained as a bright memory: he kept a locket containing a lock of Fanny's hair.

He revisited the Abbey 35 years after the break up and wrote this poem.

Discuss these questions with a partner.

1 What surprises Peacock on his return to the Abbey?

2 Look at line 2. How is he like the Abbey?

3 What sights and sounds are the same after thirty-five years?

4 What is different?

5 Explain the **simile** of the bridge. What two things does it join?

6 How does he recall the girl in memory?

7 Pick out the **antitheses** in the last two lines. What do they say about his love affair?

8 Is he bitter or sad or resigned in his memories?

NEWARK ABBEY

I gaze where August's sunbeam falls
Along these gray and lonely walls,
Till in its light absorbed appears
The lapse of five-and-thirty years.

If change there be, I trace it not
In all this consecrated spot:
No new imprint of Ruin's march
On roofless wall and frameless arch:
The woods, the hills, the fields, the stream,
Are basking in the self-same beam:
The fall, that turns the unseen mill,
As then it murmured, murmurs still.
It seems as if in one were cast
The present and the imaged past;
Spanning, as with a bridge sublime,
That awful lapse of human time;
That gulf, unfathomably spread
Between the living and the dead.

For all too well my spirit feels
The only change this scene reveals.
The sunbeams play, the breezes stir,
Unseen, unfelt, unheard by her,
Who, on that long-past August day,
Beheld with me these ruins gray.

Whatever span the fates allow,
Ere I shall be as she is now,
Still, in my bosom's inmost cell,
Shall that deep-treasured memory dwell;
That, more than language can express,
Pure miracle of loveliness,
Whose voice so sweet, whose eyes so bright,
Were my soul's music, and its light,
In those blest days when life was new,
And hope was false, but love was true.

Vocabulary

unfathomably: too deep to measure

ere: before

bosom: heart

Thomas Hardy (1840–1928) met his future wife Emma in Cornwall where he, as a young architect, had gone to restore St Juliot church. She was the Rector's sister-in-law. Their romantic courtship was set against the wonderful coast and countryside of north Cornwall. Their married happiness did not last and they became estranged. But Emma's death in 1912 made Hardy recall their first joy in each other. He revisited Cornwall and wrote a long series of poems about Emma. Read the poem and write answers to the questions.

Vocabulary

town: Launceston	
mead: field	
wan: pale	
wistlessness: state of being forgotten	
norward: from the north	

THE VOICE

Woman much missed, how you call to, call to me,
Saying that now you are not as you were
When you had changed from the one who was all to me,
But as at first, when our day was fair.

Can it be you that I hear? Let me view you, then,
Standing as when I drew near to the town
Where you would wait for me: yes, as I knew you then,
Even to the original air-blue gown!

Or is it only the breeze, in its listlessness
Travelling across the wet mead to me here,
You being ever dissolved to wan wistlessness,
Heard no more again far or near?

Thus I; faltering forward,
Leaves around me falling,
Wind oozing thin through the thorn from norward,
And the woman calling.

1 The poet thinks he hears the voice of Emma calling him. What is she saying?

2 He imagines her as she was as she waited at Launceston station. What detail of her appearance does he recall?

3 Is it really a voice calling? What else could it be?

4 Which words show his sadness in the third **stanza**?

5 What happens to the ghostly wife?

6 The smooth, waltz-like **rhythm**, with its unusual three-**syllable** rhyme (call to me/all to me), breaks down in the fourth stanza. Short jagged lines show old Hardy alone. What do his surroundings suggest about his future?

7 What does the last line mean?

Review

Return to the idea of pathetic fallacy mentioned in the introduction. Can you see any signs of it in the poems by Peacock and Hardy? Share your ideas with the class.

Homework

1 Write the story of Peacock's relationship of 1807, written perhaps as diary entries or letters. Your narrative could be based on two contrasted meetings, one happy, one sad, at the Abbey. Include Peacock's later visit as a tailpiece.

2 Compare and contrast the two poems:
   - their stories
   - their memory pictures
   - their imagery and rhythm.

3 Create, as a poem or in prose, your own remembered place that is connected with something in your life.

City exiles

Aims

- To consider poets' perspectives in texts from different cultures.
- To compare the themes and styles of these poets.

Starter session

Cities are wonderful to visit as a tourist, or to live in if you are rich. Some people are forced to move to cities to find work. Others even have to migrate from a poor country to a rich one to survive. What are the pleasures of city life for the rich? What are its horrors and dangers for poor immigrants? Write four parts on each and then discuss them as a class.

Introduction

A West Indian immigrant is the central figure of 'Island man' by Grace Nichols (b 1950). The poem is addressed to 'a Caribbean island man in London who still wakes up to the sound of the sea'.

What two places contrast here? Which words and ideas show that the man loves one and hates the other?

Vocabulary

North Circular: major road in North London

ISLAND MAN

Morning
and island man wakes up
to the sound of blue surf
in his head
the steady breaking and wombing

wild seabirds
and fishermen pushing out to sea
the sun surfacing defiantly
from the east
of his small emerald island
he always comes back
                              groggily groggily

Comes back to sands
of a grey metallic soar

                    to surge of wheels
to dull North Circular roar

muffling muffling
his crumpled pillow waves
island man heaves himself

Another London day

Development

Here are two more poems about people who have moved into cities and live in a kind of exile.

Grace Nichols was born in Guyana, West Indies and emigrated to England in 1977. She understands the stress of moving from a simple way of life on a beautiful island to an English city.

TWO OLD BLACK MEN ON A LEICESTER SQUARE PARK BENCH

What do you dream of you
old black men sitting
on park benches staunchly
wrapped up in scarves
and coats of silence
eyes far away from the cold
grey and strutting
pigeon
ashy fingers trembling
(though it's said that the old
hardly ever feel the cold)

do you dream revolutions
you could have forged
or mourn
some sunfull woman you
might have known a
hibiscus flower
ghost memories of desire

Oh it's easy
to rainbow the past
after all the letters from
home spoke of hardships

and the sun was traded long ago

Carol Ann Duffy (b 1955) has been described as 'the representative poet of the present day'. She has a particular sympathy for social outcasts. In 'Foreign', she forces us to thinks about a typical contemporary figure, a poor immigrant looking for a more prosperous life in a Western city.

FOREIGN

Imagine living in a strange, dark city for twenty years.
There are some dismal dwellings on the east side
and one of them is yours. On the landing, you hear
your foreign accent echo down the stairs. You think
in a language of your own and talk in theirs.

Then you are writing home. The voice in your head
recites the letter in a local dialect; behind that
is the sound of your mother singing to you,
all that time ago, and now you do not know
why your eyes are watering and what's the word for this.

You use the public transport. Work. Sleep. Imagine one night
you saw a name for yourself sprayed in red
against a brick wall. A hate name. Red like blood.
It is snowing on the streets, under the neon lights,
as if this place were coming to bits before your eyes.

And in the delicatessen, from time to time, the coins
in your palm will not translate. Inarticulate,
because this is not home, you point at fruit. Imagine
that one of you says *Me not know what these people mean.*
It like they only go to bed and dream. Imagine that.

'Two old black men'

1 Why does the poet pity the two black men?

2 What does the 'grey and strutting pigeon' represent?

3 What two things might the men be day dreaming about on the bench?

4 What does 'rainbow the past' mean? What have they forgotten about home?

5 How did they 'trade the sun' in their lives?

'Foreign'

6 What sort of life does the immigrant live? What does she/he dislike about the city?

7 What frightens her/him? What does she/he remember about home?

8 What effect do these memories have?

9 Why is the language problem so important in this poem?

Compare and contrast

10 How is the city represented in each poem?

11 How do the immigrants think of the past?

12 What problems of immigrant life are shown in both poems?

13 Which poem is stronger and more convincing?

Review

Which of the two poems in this section has made most impact on you? Offer your ideas to the class but refer closely to details of the poems.

Homework

1 Compose your own two-part poem, the first about the peace and beauty of country, river or sea, and the second about the crowding and noise of the city.

2 Compose the letter that the immigrant in 'Foreign' writes home. It is frank, and includes the fears, problems and emotions mentioned in the poem.

3 Write a poem or short prose sketch about a city exile hating the streets and longing for home.

Warnings

Aims

- To consider writers' perspectives in poems from different cultures.
- To compare their presentation of ideas, values and emotions.

Starter session

Most of us live in reasonable comfort in twenty-first-century Britain. What dangers can you see in the world that may undermine this security in coming years? With a partner, list ten of them. (Examples: pollution leading to climate change, terrorist strikes, etc.) Then discuss them briefly as a class.

Introduction

Wilfred Owen, the war poet, claimed that 'All a poet can do today is warn'. Roy Fuller (1921–1991) follows up these ideas, making us look at our present comfortable lives and warning us of possible threats. Think about these ideas. What does he tell us about his present 'benign routines'? What glimpse of a possible future does he offer? Who might the 'crowding visitors' be? What might cause them to come?

HAPPINESS

Some say this is a golden age,
That never again
Will there be such a deal to eat,
Such space between the race of men.

My day's benign routines incline
To such belief
However startling, since it's sure
In time (and more than likely brief)

One will awaken not to eggs,
And isolation
In gardens, but a bed of crowding
Visitors, and emaciation.

Vocabulary

benign: gentle;

emaciation: being thin through illness or starvation

Development

Elizabeth Daryush (1887–1977) is increasingly admired as a poet. Like Fuller, she sees us as living in a 'golden age' threatened with collapse. We are the 'children of wealth' she describes. Read the poem and discuss the questions in a small group.

Vocabulary

citadel: place of security

skin too white: skin which is too white

glass of comfort: the window

CHILDREN OF WEALTH

Children of wealth in your warm nursery,
Set in the cushioned window-seat to watch
The volleying snow, guarded invisibly
By the clear double pane through which no touch
Untimely penetrates, you cannot tell
What winter means; its cruel truths to you
Are only sound and sight; your citadel
Is safe from feeling, and from knowledge too.

Go down, go out to elemental wrong,
Waste your too round limbs, tan your skin too white;
The glass of comfort, ignorance, seem strong
Today, and yet perhaps this very night

You'll wake to horror's wrecking fire—your home
Is wired within for this, in every room.

People of the Western world are compared, by extended metaphor, to children who live in an over-protected environment.

1 Which words express this comfort and security?
2 What is represented by the winter weather outside?
3 What is included in 'elemental wrong'?
4 Why is the house bad for the 'children'?
5 What should they do to change their over-protected lives?
6 The threat to their lives might not come from outside: it might be within the 'house' itself. What do the last three lines mean? What dangers might be included in the faulty wiring of the 'house'?

Terrorism might be part of Daryush's 'bad wiring'. Terrorists kill, upset, and cause panic but they actually change very little.

Wislawa Szymborska (b 1923) is a Polish poet who won the Nobel Prize for Literature in 1996. She looks into the morbid mind of a terrorist with its contempt for people, its apparent power over life and death, and pleasure in the drama it is making. Read the poem and write answers to the questions.

1 How does the poet use time references to make drama?

2 We watch the terrorist crossing the street but we are also in his mind. Mostly he despises his victims but is there anywhere that he shows:
   - Brief pity for someone
   - The stress of waiting?

3 What are his motives for planting this bomb?

THE TERRORIST, HE'S WATCHING

The bomb in the bar will explode at thirteen twenty.
Now it's just thirteen sixteen.
There's still time for some to go in,
and some to come out.

The terrorist has already crossed the street.
The distance keeps him out of danger,
and what a view – just like the movies:

A woman in a yellow jacket, she's going in.
A man in dark glasses, he's coming out.
Teenagers in jeans, they're talking.
Thirteen seventeen and four seconds.
The short one, he's lucky, he's getting on a scooter,
but the tall one, he's going in.

Thirteen seventeen and forty seconds.
That girl, she's walking along with a green ribbon in her
    hair.
But then a bus suddenly pulls in front of her.
Thirteen eighteen.
The girl's gone.
Was she that dumb, did she go in or not,
we'll see when they carry them out.

Thirteen nineteen.
Somehow no one's going in.
Another guy, fat, bald, is leaving, though.
Wait a second, looks like he's looking for something in his
    pockets and
at thirteen twenty minus ten seconds
he goes back in for his crummy gloves.

Thirteen twenty exactly.
This waiting, it's taking forever.
Any second now.
No, not yet.
Yes, now.
The bomb, it explodes.

> **Vocabulary**
>
> *dumb:* stupid

Review

Look back at the list of dangers you made in the starter. Which of them are brought most vividly alive in the poems in this lesson? Discuss with the class.

Homework

1 Write three short reports:
   - One from the radio, TV or newspaper describing the bomb blast
   - One from the terrorist group saying why it carried out the attack
   - One from the terrorist's diary, describing his feelings as he waited for the bomb to go off.

2 Write an **acrostic poem** based on the word WARNINGS. Include some of your previously-listed threats to the modern world.

Glossary

Word	Unit	Page	Definition
Abstract idea	9/1	78	An idea, imagined in the mind, that does not actually exist (for example, fear, beauty).
Acrostic poem	9/9	110	A poem made by writing a word in capitals down the page. Then each initial letter is taken to begin a line.
Adjective	7/1	9	A word that describes or modifies a noun.
Adverb	7/3	16	A word that describes or modifies a verb.
Alliteration	7/4	20	The repetition of similar **consonant** sounds, especially at the beginning of words that are used close to each other.
Ambiguous (noun: ambiguity)	8/6	56	A word or expression that carries more than one meaning.
Antithesis	9/8	101	A clash of strongly contrasted words.
Atmosphere	7/3	16	The feeling or mood created in the mind by a place or **setting**.
Ballad	7/2	10	A simple **narrative poem**. Each four-line **stanza** contains a **refrain**. It is intended to be sung or chanted.
Colloquial	9/4	90	Language that sounds like everyday, familiar speech.
Comparison	7/1	9	Saying that one thing is like another. Poetic **imagery** is the technical name for this.
Consonant			Every letter of the alphabet except the **vowels** a, e, i, o, u.
Couplet	8/10	75	Two rhymed lines of verse, particularly at the end of a **sonnet**.
Dialogue	9/4	87	A conversation between two or more people.
Diction	7/1	9	The poet's choice and use of words.
Elegy (adjective: elegiac)	8/5	57	A sad poem or song mourning someone's death.
Emotive language	7/5	24	Words that create strong feeling.
Epigram (adjective: epigrammatic)	9/6	96	A short poem containing a clever or surprising thought. It can be **satirical**.
Epitaph	7/5	23	A piece of writing about a dead person.
Extended metaphor	9/1	78	A suggested **comparison** that is carried on at length, perhaps right through a poem.
Foot			A pair or group of **syllables** making up a unit in the poem's **meter**.
Free verse	8/8	70	It does not follow the usual verse forms or meters. Each line is a statement with no regular rhythm. When the statement is finished, whether long or short, a new line begins. It gives the impression of quick, spontaneous thought.
Imagery	9/4	87	The technical word for the various kinds of **comparisons** made in poems (mostly **simile** or **metaphor**).
Irony (adjective: ironic)	8/1	44	A humorous or slightly sarcastic use of words to imply the opposite of what they normally mean.
Lyric	8/9	72	A short poem expressing thoughts and feelings.
Manuscript	7/4	18	The hand-written (or typed) first copy of a poem.

Word	Unit	Page	Definition
Metaphor	7/1	9	An indirect or suggested comparison.
Meter	8/10	75	The way in which verse is arranged in patterns, using stressed or unstressed syllables which make up poetic feet. Different meters have different names that describe the number of feet in the line, for example, tetrameter (4), pentameter (5) or hexameter (6).
Narrative poem	7/2	10	A poem that tells a story.
Octet (or octave)	8/1	44	The first eight-line section of an Italian **sonnet**.
Pathetic fallacy	9/7	100	Where landscapes and objects, that are not alive, are shown as having, or reflecting, human feelings or moods.
Pentameter	8/10	75	A poetic line of five **feet** (each one having an **unstressed** and **stressed syllable** in it). It is the most common **meter** in English poetry.
Phrase	7/4	20	A group of words that contains an idea (but not a complete verb) and is part of a sentence.
Poet Laureate	7/8	34	The official poet to the British King or Queen.
Pun	7/10	40	A joke or play on words involving the use of more than one meaning in a word, or of a word that sounds like another.
Quatrain	8/10	75	A group of four lines of verse which may be rhymed or unrhymed.
Refrain			A chorus that is repeated, often at the end of a stanza.
Rhyme	7/6	25	Words that rhyme end with the same sound. Usually the **vowels** in rhyming words are the same, and the **consonants** are different, for example, cold/sold.
Rhyme scheme	7/2	10	The pattern of line-ending rhymes in a poem. You mark them ABAB, CDCD, etc.
Rhythm	7/2	10	The beat of a line of poetry.
Satirical (noun: satire)			Attacking ideas, people or society by mockery.
Sequence	8/5	57	A series of poems that are loosely connected together.
Setting	7/3	14	The time and place described in a poem.
Sestet	8/1	44	The last six-line section of an Italian sonnet.
Simile	8/4	55	A direct comparison that starts with 'like' or 'as'.
Sonnet	8/10	75	A fourteen-line poem in **pentameter rhythm** with a **rhyme scheme** of various patterns. The two most important are Italian (8 + 6) and English (4 + 4+ 4 + 2).
Stanza	7/2	10	A verse or group of lines that form a unit.
Stress	7/2	10	The syllable given most emphasis in a poetic **foot**. It is usually marked (/).
Style	7/6	27	The way in which a writer expresses an idea.
Syllable	8/10	75	A separate sound within a word (for example, 'independent' has four syllables).
Theme	7/2	10	The general idea developed in a poem.
Unstressed	8/10	75	The syllable given less emphasis in a poetic foot. It is usually marked (u).
Verb	7/1	9	A word that defines an action or a state (a doing or being word).
Verse form	7/2	10	The shape and pattern of lines or **stanzas** in a poem.
Vowels			The letters a, e, i, o, u.